THE COMPLETE
WILDFOWLER

THE COMPLETE WILDFOWLER

by Grits Gresham

Foreword by Dr. Leslie L. Glasgow

WINCHESTER PRESS

Library of Congress Catalog Card Number: 73–78827
ISBN: 0–87691–118–1

Published by Winchester Press
460 Park Avenue, New York 10022

Printed in the United States of America

Contents

Preface

A glance at the table of contents quickly reveals that *The Complete Wildfowler* covers wildfowling from A to Z. And after reading the book, it is equally obvious that it was written by an expert who is both scientist and gunner.

Grits Gresham is one of those rare individuals who has both an advanced degree in Wildlife Management and many years' experience as a professional outdoor writer. This unusual combination of education and experience has resulted in a book that is not only very delightful reading but is also technically correct.

Waterfowl hunters are much more knowledgeable these days but otherwise have changed little since the sport of fowling began. They display the same eternal enthusiasm and interest as their predecessors. Their day is still the same: up in the wee hours of the morning; black coffee and hot biscuits; hip boots and hunting jacket; duck call and decoys; shell box and shotgun; retriever and guide followed by an exhilarating ride to the blind. And the same intense anticipation as dawn breaks and wings whistle in the fog. And after the hunt is over, the fine camp meals, toasts to a great day in the blind, and the evening comradeship with people who love duck hunting.

But although hunters have changed little, there has been a radical change in harvest regulations and in the condition of waterfowl habitat. Regulations are more complicated and habitat has deteriorated acutely.

Bag limits have been lowered, partly because of an increase in the number of waterfowl hunters, but more importantly because of the loss of breeding habitat and in some instances wintering habitat.

In order to perpetuate hunting and to permit less restrictive bag limits, new harvest regulations are being tested and some are now ready for adoption. Species management, bonus ducks, complete prohibition on shooting some species, early teal seasons, and zoning to harvest local nonmigratory populations have already passed the experimental stage and are now considered normal management practices. The point system is on the verge of being adopted and will very likely become commonplace.

These novel regulations are designed to protect the resource and at the same time provide the gunner with a more liberal bag. Since they are more complicated than previous regulations, the waterfowler must become more sophisticated.

Because of the excellent educational programs of state game commissions, the U.S. Bureau of Sports Fisheries and Wildlife, and Ducks Unlimited, many hunters can identify waterfowl by species and by sex, in the hand and frequently in flight; they know a great deal about waterfowl biology and understand the major management problems. This increased knowledge is a source of great satisfaction to the hunter and an aid to better waterfowl management.

Every waterfowler is saddened by the drastic decline in habitat condition and acreage. Although damage has been done by damming and filling, the most drastic loss of habitat has resulted largely from channelization and drainage programs carried out by the U.S. Soil Conservation Service, the U.S. Army Corps of Engineers and state public-works departments. Most of the damage has been done at public expense, and even the waterfowl hunter has been compelled to help pay for it through his tax dollar.

Despite the tremendous effort by state game commissioners, by the U.S. Bureau of Sports Fisheries and Wildlife, by Ducks Unlimited and by private hunting clubs, the future of waterfowl habitat looks dim indeed! In order to save the sport of wildfowling, every hunter should put forth relentless effort toward saving habitat.

I am sure this book will make a valuable contribution toward this end and also to the hunter's knowledge of waterfowl and the pleasure he finds in fowling.

–DR. LESLIE L. GLASGOW
School of Forestry and Wildlife Management
LOUISIANA STATE UNIVERSITY

Chapter 1

What It's All About

WIND-DRIVEN SNOW and sleet cut visibility on Currituck Sound to less than half a mile, but the pair of hunters in the ice-crusted blind forgot the elements when they spotted a faint dark line which said ducks. Peering across the water, they watched the flock of bluebills finally swing back into the wind, committed to their decoys.

Three thousand miles away another pair of gunners, their shirt-sleeved forms concealed in mosquito-netting camouflage, froze into immobility as a flight of pintails warily circled their Sacramento Valley ricefield blind. Hearing a familiar whistle coming from the lifelike stool and suddenly deciding that all was right, the graceful ducks heeled over and headed in. They were almost within range when a shot rang out from a blind far across the field, and they towered to safety. "Damn!"

Far south, in the mangrove lagoons of the Yucatan Peninsula, the Mayan guide and his hunter came up shooting as
a tightly packed knot of blue-winged teal poured between the

*Don't move! The moment of truth approaches as two geese head on in. Discipline
is the name of the game for the gunner, since he must not make his move too
soon. This is one of the most exciting moments in waterfowling.*

trees at flank speed. *"Bueno! Bueno!"* the Mayan cried and broke into a tooth-filled grin as a pair of the ducks crumpled to the water.

Led by a veteran of many migrations, the flock of blue and snow geese rose from the sanctuary of its roosting reservoir and headed across the southeast Texas ricefields to feed. The wise leader carefully nursed the group between and around the many blind-decoy setups down below, although she had to speak harshly at times to keep the birds in line. Then, just before beginning a letdown into the refuge, two youngsters succumbed to hunger and the pleadings from the ground and coasted downward toward the waiting guns.

From Florida to Washington, Mexico to Manitoba, North Carolina to California, the words are different but the song is the same. The thrill of duck and goose hunting spans the length and breadth of this continent, and comes in a sufficient variety of shapes and sizes to satisfy the most discriminating gunner. To many of us, the heritage of waterfowling is the greatest outdoor legacy we have.

The sport can be simple and inexpensive. A careful stroll along just about any creek bottom in many states will afford jump shooting at the beautiful wood duck. Consider the farm youngster with his single-barrel, stalking transient ducks resting on this stock pond—he is a genuine gunner, and there are thousands of him.

Yes, the sport *can* be simple and inexpensive, but more often it isn't. Duck and goose shooting characteristically demand a considerable quantity of equipment, planning and knowledge. In this very complexity lies much of its appeal, for our nation is one in which the challenge of the difficult is a call to arms.

How else can you explain the phenomenon of thousands of men rising from their warm beds hours before dawn, traveling countless miles by car, boat and on foot through subfreezing weather, to try to bag . . . two ducks. That's the way

Waterfowling can be simple, but usually isn't. Duck shooting such as this, for instance, requires boats, decoys, hip boots or waders, blind, duck call and the ability to use it, and, of course, shotgun and shells.

it was in the 1962–63 hunting season, when gunners in the Mississippi Flyway were permitted only two ducks per day in the bag.

To the avid waterfowler, no moment of truth can match the instant when a flock first responds to his call and decoys, the time when this wild, free bird of unsurpassed grace begins a descent from the sky down to gun range. It is a stirring spectacle of nature which, once experienced, usually haunts a man for life.

Yet there is much more to waterfowl hunting than the shooting. The comradeship of hunting companions, the closeness to nature demanded by the sport, the contact with so many water-loving creatures, and the satisfaction of coping with adverse weather all play their roles. Modern bag limits make absurd the theory that the waterfowler hunts to put meat in the pot. It's the hunting, not the killing, that grabs him and holds him.

Climbing out of the goose pit to stretch was disastrous for these two gunners, since this flock of Canada geese chose the same moment for their appearance. The unexpected seems to occur frequently in waterfowl hunting, and is a delightful part of what it's all about.

Though there is infinitely more to the sport of wildfowling than the killing, there is no denying the fact that shooting is a vital, necessary part of the drama. The bag may be light or nonexistent, but anticipation of the opportunity to shoot must be present.

But there is no denying the fact that the princely sport of waterfowling *demands* the shooting. The exquisitely satisfying drama is incomplete until you pull the trigger, until recoil tells you that the graceful tool in your hands has come alive, until the pungent aroma of burned gunpowder fills the crisp air. Until a well-placed charge of shot stills flaring wings—or until a not-so-well-placed volley furnishes a futile salute for a fast-disappearing, unscathed flock.

There must be, in other words, reasonable opportunity to shoot, or the anticipation of this opportunity, before hunters will make the effort or stand the expense that duck or goose hunting requires. If shooting were not such a vital part of hunting, men would visit their duck blinds before and after the season, as well as during it, but without their guns, enjoying their communion with the great outdoors. That does not happen with any frequency.

More than two million men and women in the United States alone are waterfowlers. They are a breed apart, a rather large "small segment" of a total hunting population of over twenty million.

No group of gunners is more dedicated to their particular brand of outdoor sport, and no group has gone to greater lengths to ensure the perpetuation of it. With zeal and enthusiasm they have given of their time, their energies and their money in an effort to make sure that ducks, geese and other wildfowl will be with us forever.

Waterfowlers have a fierce desire to make sure that duck- and goose-hunting opportunities remain a significant chapter in the American sporting scene. For the remainder of their hunting lives, and for their children and their grandchildren. Forever.

They know that if we ever reach the point where nobody may experience the sweet thrills of wildfowling, the unique flavor of shooting ducks and geese, then this country will have lost a precious heritage. An irreplaceable era will have ended.

They love the sport of waterfowling, and very simply, that's what it's all about.

A big flock of blue and snow geese mills over a Louisiana marsh, in typical blue-snow "goose fashion." They frequently do exactly that for minutes at a time before deciding to settle down for a landing . . . or to go elsewhere.

Chapter 2

Ducks and Geese

"THE HOMEBOUND SPORTSMAN unable to name the ducks slung over his shoulder is an anachronism, a relic of that I-got-my-limit era which nearly ruined the continent and its resources."

Aldo Leopold, Professor of Wildlife Management at the University of Wisconsin, wrote that in his introduction to *The Ducks, Geese and Swans of North America,* a superb book written by Francis H. Kortright and first published in 1942. It contains a vast array of information about the life history of each species of waterfowl found on this continent, plus a set of paintings and illustrations by T. M. Shortt which are superior as identification aids. The ducks are shown not only in all the splendor of their spring plumages, but also in their autumn garb, which frequently puzzles hunters.

Did you know that all ducks become completely flightless for a period of time each summer? Unless you live in an area in which ducks nest there is a good chance that you didn't, but it's a fact. The reason is that, unlike most birds, ducks molt their flight feathers all at the same time. For a period of several weeks, until those flight feathers grow back, they can't fly at all.

And did you know that those colorful males, including that jaunty greenhead, molt into an "eclipse" plumage which very closely resembles the drab appearance of the females? It happens in summer, interestingly enough, when they need all the camouflage protection possible during that flightless period. It's another splendid example of the workings of nature.

Such facts are among the many in Kortright's book. How much does a pintail weigh? It's there—2 pounds, 2½ ounces average for males; 1 pound, 13 ounces average for females. The facts and figures in this splendid, 476-page volume are almost endless. Especially good are the "field marks" descriptions, both on the water and in flight.

Identifying a duck or goose should be divided into three forms. "In flight" is perhaps most important to the gunner in these days of species regulations, and is the one requiring most study and practice in order to gain proficiency. "On the water" is quite another, with the bird sitting quietly, preferably at close range, where all form and color characteristics can be observed. The third form is a "bird in the hand"—a shapeless, inert bundle of feathers, sometimes very difficult to identify.

When a duck is on the wing, factors other than just its appearance can be very meaningful in identification. Consider Kortright's description of the mallard: "Not particularly rapid; the head and neck are carried pointed slightly upward; the body appears large and the wing spread is ample." Then he goes to the look of the bird: "In flight, the foreparts and hindquarters of the male appear dark, the breast and underwing surface show white, and the two white bars of the specu-

Most popular duck species with gunners is the mallard, which tops the harvest list in all four flyways. In the 1972 season mallards made up almost one-fourth of the kill in the Atlantic Flyway, and about 45 percent in the Central Flyway.

lum are very evident. The female can be identified on the wing by the *two* white bars of the speculum and the white underwing surface. The female pintail is similar, but its neck is longer, tail more pointed, and the white wing-bars and white wing-lining are lacking."

This invaluable book is available from the Wildlife Management Institute, 709 Wire Building, Washington, D.C. 20005. A copy of it belongs in the library of any avid waterfowler, even if it's a one-volume library.

Aldo Leopold was telling it like it is in his introduction to the book. The hunter who isn't concerned or interested in what kind of duck or goose he hunts or shoots, or in properly identifying it after he kills it, doesn't deserve the pleasure of waterfowling. His attitude is an affront to the marvelous creatures he shoots, and to other gunners.

Rapid identification of ducks on the wing cannot be faultlessly certain. Under good conditions an expert won't make many mistakes, but in the gray light of dawn his task is magnified. The average hunter, under most conditions, can train himself to identify the most popular and abundant ducks in his area most of the time. After he has killed a bird, he should be able to identify it in all but the exceptional instance. What separates him from the who-cares-what-it-is class of hunter is that he'll try to identify any unknown bird in some manner, and the next time around he'll know it.

This chapter is only an introduction to wildfowl identification. The gunner who wants to achieve proficiency will require a good field guide (several are recommended at the end of the chapter) and some practical experience.

During the time of year when hunting seasons are open, the females of some species are rather easily confused with each other. Alleviating that problem is the fact that most species fly in flocks of their own kind, and thus the more readily recognizable males in the flock are the key to identifying the females.

There are certain characteristics of waterfowl which quickly become of importance in identification. Virtually all of the popular ducks are separated into two groups: diving ducks, such as the redhead, canvasback, scaup and ringnecks; and puddle ducks (river and pond ducks, in Kortright's vernacular), which are the surface-feeders such as the mallard, pintail, gadwall and baldpate.

If a flock of approaching birds flies like diving ducks—typically in a tightly packed grouping which proceeds swiftly and directly on its path—the hunter mentally eliminates the puddle-duck species from his identification puzzle. If the flock is loosely knit and scattered, tending to circle and wander, he eliminates diving ducks.

The rule isn't foolproof. Teal are puddle ducks, but fly in

dense, compact flocks which twist and turn. So do scaup, which are diving ducks, but the almost incessant twittering and chirping of teal differentiate them from scaup.

The maneuvers of a flock in the air, therefore, are a great aid in identification. So are such things as sound, of both voice and wings; silhouette, shape and color; method of feeding; and landing and takeoff characteristics.

Puddle ducks spring vertically into the air on takeoff, and land much as would a helicopter, zooming deliberately in and

One of the least popular duck species is the shoveler, since many gunners erroneously believe that they aren't good table fare. Here a gaudy shoveler drake, left, and two females "fly" their way out of the water. It's a typical takeoff of puddle ducks, which bounce, spring or fly their way vertically into the air.

settling to the water. Diving ducks usually "run" along the water on takeoff, and land with a rush.

Puddle ducks are usually found in fresh, shallow marshes. Divers frequent the larger, deeper lakes and rivers and coastal bays. Although puddle ducks are good divers, they usually feed in very shallow water just by dabbling or tipping. Divers feed most of the time by diving, sometimes to great depths. Ducks feeding on croplands are almost sure to be puddle ducks, since they can handle themselves well on land.

Management of waterfowl has moved more and more to species distinctions in the past decade, with the goal of permitting greater utilization of those birds in good supply and giving greater protection to those in short supply. It is a sound trend, but places upon the hunter the burden of identification. He must be able to recognize species in order to know what he may legally shoot and what he may not.

Years ago I was tremendously impressed by a duck guide who could instantly give the name, rank and serial number of any flock which happened past. "Gadwall!" he would tersely answer when I asked the identity of a lone bird off in the distance. Or "Mostly mallards with a few pintails in with 'em," he would say of a moving smudge on the horizon.

Finally I could stand it no longer, and asked him the secret of his marvelous powers. The secret, he finally revealed, was the fact that the birds weren't going to come close enough for anybody to know whether he was right or not.

When you get a flock in over the decoys, over your gun barrel, that kind of identification isn't good enough. Then you had best be sure of your target. The worst part of an error at that time is that you might shoot a species under complete protection, as the canvasback and redhead were in most flyways during the 1972–73 season. The least of it could be that you shoot a high-point duck which completes your daily limit, ending your gunning for that day.

For the thirteen species of ducks which are most significant in the hunter's bag, I will list some key points to use in making

The greater Canada goose is the largest of the geese, and is in good population status. Despite that, the scene shown here—three Canadas settling into decoys in a Louisiana marsh—hasn't been repeated for more than five years. Shortstopping farther up the Mississippi Flyway has effectively ended the migration of Canadas into Louisiana and Arkansas, where the season on these birds has been closed for some five years.

an in-flight identification, keeping in mind the general group and flock characteristics mentioned above.

I will also list keys for the four species of geese which are important to hunters—Canada, snow, blue, and white-fronted. Identification is much easier for geese than for ducks. Both physical appearance and voice are sufficient to pinpoint geese for the knowledgeable wildfowler.

Ducks

MALLARD *(greenhead)* · Flight not particularly fast, with a leisurely wingbeat. Flies with head and neck pointed slightly upward. A big duck, with ample wingspread. Foreparts and hindquarters of male appear dark with breast and underwing surface showing white. Two white bars of speculum prominent. Female: *two* white bars and white underwing surface.

BLACK DUCK *(black mallard)* · Usually in small flocks, flying swiftly and high, in V's or angular lines. Shy and wary. Large, *very dark* bodies contrast to silvery underwing surfaces. Sexes alike.

MOTTLED DUCK · Almost identical to black duck, except body is lighter in color.

PINTAIL *(sprig)* · Long "pin" tail, pointed wings, and white neck and breast of the males are keys. Graceful; with long necks stretched out and long tails they are distinctive. Females resemble female mallard, but have pointed tail and no white wing-bars or white wing-lining. Whistle of drakes, which is constant in flock of any size.

GADWALL *(gray duck)* · White patch on speculum of both sexes, prominent in flying birds, is key. No other puddle duck has it. (White wing patch on baldpate is on forepart of wing, not speculum.) Black rump of male.

BALDPATE *(widgeon)* · White crown and breast of drakes very conspicious. Also, white patch on forewing. Females show white breast, whitish wing patch. No white in speculum of male or female. Voice distinctive, a whistling *"whew-whew-whew"* repeated constantly.

TEAL · It is very difficult to separate blue-wings from green-wings except at close range (or with binoculars) in good light. Very fast and very small. Tight formations, twisting and turning. In good light the blue wing patch of the blue-winged teal is prominent.

SHOVELER *(spoony, spoonbill)* · Male is strikingly marked, from below as alternating black and white. Huge distinctive bill and short neck in both sexes. Blue wing patch on both. Head and neck carried in downward slope when in flight.

WOOD DUCK *(woodie)* · Flight swift and direct, with head held high, above level of body, *but with bill pointed downward* (which separates it from baldpate, even at a distance). Dark chest of male contrasts with white breast and long, dark tail. Voice is unmistakable.

SCAUP, GREATER AND LESSER *(bluebill)* · Most important diving duck in bag. Flight swift and erratic, often in large, compact flocks. Males white in the middle and black on both ends. White speculum on male and female. White mask on female at base of bill.

RING-NECKED DUCK *(ringbill)* · Similar to scaup, but has no white speculum. Usually fly in small open-formation flocks.

CANVASBACK *(can)* · That "canvas back" is a key: the body is white. A very big duck, long and slender, with dark head, neck and tail. Wingbeat rapid. Females darker. Sloping "ski-nose" forehead of both sexes is prominent and distinctive.

REDHEAD · Similar to canvasback, but has round head shape and appears shorter and darker in flight. Very rapid wingbeat and erratic flight. Male has gray back (can has white back) and white breast. Female has brown back, and is often difficult to separate from female scaup (which has white face patch) and ring-necked duck (which has a white ring around the eye).

Geese

CANADA GOOSE *(honker)* · Gray body and long black neck. White cheek patch. Fly with long necks outstretched in a slight downward curve. All subspecies look alike, varying only in size. Unmistakable. Loud, resonant, two-part honk is giveaway to common Canada. Voice of lesser Canada equally distinctive, similar but higher-pitched.

Canada geese come in an assortment of sizes. The greater Canada will weigh from 10 to 15 pounds, while the lesser Canada isn't much larger than a mallard.

PHOTO COURTESY U.S. DEPARTMENT OF THE INTERIOR

The white face patch is a distinctive identifying mark of the Canada geese, and both sexes look alike. This pair was banded by the Bureau of Sport Fisheries and Wildlife in Alaska.

WHITE-FRONTED GOOSE *(specklebelly)* · Voice very distinctive, completely different from other geese. Described as an often-repeated, laughing cackle. Whitish breast splashed irregularly with black or brown markings, and white band around face at base of bill, from which it derives its name.

A glance at this white-fronted goose will tell why the species is commonly called the "specklebelly." One of the wariest of the geese, it ranks at the top with epicures.

BLUE GOOSE · White head and neck and dark-blue body are unmistakable. Immature birds have brownish heads and necks during first autumn. Voice is high-pitched, sharp and distinctive.

LESSER SNOW GOOSE · Snow-white, with black wing

tips. Shrill voice is distinctive. Snows and blues frequently fly together.

Although these seventeen species are by far the most important to the hunter on this continent, there are other interesting ones which deserve mention. The cinnamon teal is a western species which closely resembles the blue-winged teal, but the male is a cinnamon-red color with a bright-blue wing patch. West of the Rockies it can be quite common in the hunter's bag.

The goldeneye is a striking duck of medium size. The male is largely white with black on the back, and the black head is marked with a white face patch just in front of the eye. The old-squaw are sea ducks seen in the United States only around the Great Lakes and the northeast coast, and their great diving ability makes them vulnerable to being caught in fish nets. The bufflehead is one of the smallest ducks, and the huge white patch on the head of the male, extending from the eye around the back of the head, is a sure identification.

The ruddy is one of the small ones, too, and the long, stiff tail of the male, frequently cocked vertically, is distinctive. Other birds which find their way into the hunter's bag include the mergansers—the red-breasted, the American and the hooded.

Color patterns of the feathers on ducks are, of course, key identification features, but so are the colors of feet, legs and bills. Make it a point to notice these colors when you have a bird in the hand.

The female pintail, baldpate and gadwall are sometimes confused with each other. If it has yellow feet it's a gadwall. Pintails *and* baldpate have bluish-gray feet and bills, but the tip of the bill on the baldpate is *black*. This is an example of how these feet, legs and bill features can be used to separate similar-appearing species.

Small bird-identification books are called "field guides," and a field guide to waterfowl is a very handy item for all duck hunters. I frequently carry one along in my shell bucket, not only for the purpose of keying down unusual duck species I might happen across, but also to identify other non-game birds.

Best known of the guides to birds are those by Roger Tory Peterson. They are widely available, and highly recommended. Also good for identification are the unusual *Top Flight Speed Index to Waterfowl of North America* by Ruthven and Zimmerman (Moebius Printing Co., Milwaukee, Wisc.) and the paperback Golden Nature Guide volume *Gamebirds,* obtainable from most booksellers.

A very helpful booklet called "Ducks at a Distance" is available for 25 cents from the Superintendent of Documents, U.S. Government Printing Office, Washington, D.C.

Chapter 3

Other Wildfowl: Cranes, Coots, Swans, Rails and Snipe

IN THE GOLDEN years of shotgunning in North America—the second half of the last century and the first few years of this one—the variety of wildfowl available for gunning was tremendous. Ducks and geese, although a major portion of the total, were only that—a portion.

Shorebird shooting was enjoyed by many hunters, though this facet of our gunning history remains in memory largely through the old decoys salvaged from that era. Yellowlegs, plover, dowitcher, curlew, gulls, herons, egret, snipe, godwit— game birds from another age. The hunting seasons on most of these birds were closed along about 1918 "for a period of ten years." Half a century later they remain closed.

Perhaps it is appropriate that there should be no hunting

of any of these, though possibly some could provide regulated gunning pleasure at no loss to the resource. Yet it's just conceivable that some of these species would be better off today had hunting seasons on them been conducted over the past years. For after more than fifty years of complete protection from hunting, as one sportsman put it, "We are not yet neckdeep in yellowlegs and plover." His point, of course, was that gun pressure has obviously not been the total answer to a bountiful population of all of the above species. The exception is for herons and egrets, which don't cut much of a figure as game birds.

It is significant that we now know far more about the life histories, habits, habitat needs and populations of ducks and geese than we do about any of the non-huntable species. The reason is simple: the interest of hunters in proper management of game birds, and their willingness to pay for it. As one conservationist so aptly put it, "It's nice to be wanted if you're a wildlife creature." If you're a desirable game species, in other words, hunters will make sure that you prosper.

So the main waterfowl species today are ducks and geese. However, coots, rails, snipe, cranes and swans are still hunted in a few areas and the wildfowler should know something about them.

COOTS AND RAILS · These are not ducks or geese, nor do they even belong to the same family, but they are found in aquatic habitat, are in good population supply, and provide a substantial amount of gunning pleasure. The coot is technically merely a kind of rail, but its habits and appearance distinguish it from other rails.

Don't confuse the coot with the scoter, or sea duck, which is often erroneously called a coot. Coots are ducklike birds, but have a white, chickenlike bill, and toes which are lobed rather than webbed like those of ducks and geese. They are slow-flying, and get off the water only with difficulty after a taxi run across the surface.

Whistling swans are the largest of the wildfowl species on which hunting is permitted. Limited hunts are now held in Utah, Nevada, and Montana, but these four were photographed over a goose blind on the Eastern Shore of Maryland, where swans are protected.

Coots are rather abundant; about a million are shot and retrieved each season. The kill is spread across all flyways, but the Mississippi provides about half of it. Still, coots aren't held in high esteem by most duck hunters either as a winged target or on the table, so most don't bother to shoot them. They are a fitting challenge for the youngster or novice, however, and properly prepared, coots are more than just palatable. The coot has an unusually large gizzard, and "coot-gizzard gumbo" is a delicacy.

Coots are commonly seen in open water, but other rails are wading birds which inhabit marshy areas, seldom resort to swimming, and fly only with reluctance. Their bodies can be compressed laterally, allowing them to walk through thick grass and close-growing reeds.

The flight of a rail is unlike that of a coot except in one respect: it is equally poor. Rails usually lumber into the air from the marsh vegetation in a roughly vertical fashion, fly weakly for a short distance with legs dangling, and collapse back to earth. They are surprisingly easy to miss. Much of the difficulty of shooting rails lies in getting them to fly in the first place, and in being able to navigate the marshes where they live.

Most rail hunting is done along the marshes of the Eastern Seaboard and the Gulf Coast, but the gun pressure on these birds is relatively light. Poling a boat through a marsh on a very high tide was a favorite sport in bygone years in Virginia and Maryland, but little of that is done any more.

The clapper and king rails are the Big Two in size and importance, ranging from 15 to 19 inches in length. Both are excellent eating. Two other species which are on the hunting list are the sora and the Virginia, both very small birds about 8 to 10 inches long. The clapper is a bird of the salt marshes, but the other three are frequently found in both salt and freshwater marshes.

Season lengths and bag limits on rails are liberal. On coots the season usually coincides with the duck season, with more liberal bag limits.

WILSON'S SNIPE *(jacksnipe)* · This is the only member of the snipe family on which hunting is still permitted. An unfortunately prolonged closed season on this great game bird, which began following a 1939 freeze that killed many birds on the wintering grounds, effectively ended most interest in snipe hunting.

Although the complete closure of the snipe season was based on fragmentary reports of the extent of the loss, with virtually no data on snipe populations continent-wide, such total protection could be justified as a precautionary measure. Better to be safe than sorry.

Of all the wildfowl it is perhaps the snipe which affords the gunner the greatest challenge. Swift and erratic in flight, the long-beaked marsh dweller puts a premium on speed and accuracy in gun pointing.

The error was in not reopening a season on snipe until a dozen years had passed—much longer than necessary for the populations to recover completely from one bad winter. During that closed period most of the old-time snipe hunters passed from the scene, and no new ones were developed. Not very many have adopted the sport since the season was reopened two decades ago, in the fall of 1953.

Snipe are birds of the marshy areas, the edges, the wet pastures and rice fields. They are superb wing-shooting targets, fast and erratic in flight, and the few ounces of meat beneath those feathers provide an epicurean delight.

Most gunning for snipe is jump shooting, although duck hunters in marsh situations often get opportunities for shots.

SANDHILL CRANE · These have been on the agenda for wildfowlers for the past few years in parts of New Mexico and Texas, and the population of these wary birds is more than coping with gun pressure. Hunting them is much akin to goose hunting, and is done over decoys or by pass shooting.

Although hunters are learning more and more about how to hunt and call the big birds, the cranes are keeping pace by learning more about avoiding hunters. The seasons are providing a great deal of hunting recreation at little expense to the population of sandhill cranes.

To avoid any possibility of losing any of the rare whooping cranes to hunters who might mistake them for sandhills, no shooting of the sandhills is permitted in southeast or south Texas. Only in western Texas, far from the Aransas Refuge wintering grounds of the whoopers, is hunting legal.

Crane hunting is centered around the Bitter Lake Refuge near Roswell, New Mexico, and the Muleshoe Refuge near Muleshoe, Texas, but in 1972 there were also open seasons in Montana, Wyoming, North and South Dakota, Oklahoma and Colorado. Some of them aren't very significant, as witnessed by the fact that the total crane kill in the 37-day season in Wyoming was reported as two birds.

The hunting of sandhill cranes has been legal for the past few years in New Mexico and in west Texas, far from any area where this bird might be confused with the rare whooping crane. Here a hunter sets out silhouette crane decoys close to the Bitter Lake Refuge in New Mexico, near Roswell.

As an indication of just how wary and intelligent these cranes are, consider the experience of wildlife managers who were trying to trap them for banding. Working along the Platte River in Nebraska, they tried all kinds of commercial decoys—silhouettes and full bodies—with no success. Then they had a taxidermist mount two real cranes and used them alone for decoys, and the cranes came right on in, where they were captured with cannon nets. It was obvious that the wild birds could and did distinguish between artificial decoys and the real thing—even though the real thing was stuffed.

WHISTLING SWANS · Like the sandhill cranes, the whistling swans have developed a healthy enough population to support a limited, controlled season. Such a season has been held in Utah since 1962, providing a modest amount of outdoor gunning and a modest harvest of birds, again without damage to the swan population. One thousand permits, each good for only one swan, were issued each year. In 1962 the kill was 320 birds and in 1963 it was 392 birds. The wintering swan population in that north Utah area ranged from 10,000 to more than 20,000 birds.

Since that beginning the swan season has been expanded. Now it is held in Utah, with 2,500 one-bird permits issued; in one county of Nevada, 500 permits; and one county of Montana, also 500 permits. The states issue the permits on a lottery basis, but as of now the number of permits in Nevada and Montana have been about sufficient for the demand. In Utah the number of applicants is now three to four times the number of permits available.

Hunter success has been about 50 percent.

BRANG · These are actually geese, but gunning for them is so restricted and special that I place them in this chapter. They are small, scarcely larger than a mallard, with a male weighing about three pounds. Brant are birds of the sea.

The American brant is a bird of the Atlantic Coast, wintering from New Jersey down to North Carolina. The black brant is found only along the Pacific Coast. The species are very similar in appearance and nest together in some parts of the Arctic, but they seldom interbreed since they normally pair off while on wintering grounds a continent apart.

Chapter 4

Where It Happens

NORTH, SOUTH, EAST, WEST! With rare exceptions, wildfowling of some sort is found in every section of the United States, and much of Canada and Mexico. However, distribution varies widely, and water plus movement are the keys to distribution.

Most wildfowl are migratory. Twice each year they make a move, traveling a few hundred or a few thousand miles to set up housekeeping in a new part of the world. It is a behavior pattern which is as yet little understood, but one which is fortunate for the sportsman since it brings birds to many more localities than would otherwise have access to them.

Wildfowl require wetlands, but not all aquatic habitat provides their complete needs. Were it not for migration, most of these marginal areas, deficient in some respect, would be without ducks and geese. But because of the long journeys which wildfowl make each fall and each spring, virtually every bit of wetland in the nation is used by waterfowl.

When the pioneers were settling this continent, they found massive populations of wildfowl, far beyond those which exist today. The abundance and distribution of wetlands in North America—an estimated 127 million acres in the United States alone—were responsible.

As the wetlands were reduced, drained or despoiled in a variety of ways, the populations of ducks and geese and other birds which require an aquatic environment also declined. The continent is still losing wetlands, and waterfowl populations continue their overall downward direction.

The bright side of the picture, however, is that an aroused public, led by waterfowl hunters, is fighting to slow the rate of attrition of the vital marshes and ponds, and indeed to restore habitat which has been destroyed. Losses continue to exceed gains, and an accelerated effort will be required in the next few years to prevent loss of some of our most famous duck-hunting areas, but the essential point is that we have the opportunity to do just that.

Despite the losses, we still have millions of acres of wetlands, and literally thousands of excellent gunning areas. That being the case, it is obviously beyond the scope of any book even to list them all, much less describe them in any detail. Even so, some especially famous areas demand recognition. Chesapeake, Stuttgart, Merrymeeting, Currituck, Catahoula, Cairo, Bear River, Eastern Shore, Matagorda Bay, Illinois River—these and many other names are famous among waterfowlers. They conjure up visions of hip boots and pirogues, of sneak boats and duck calls, of frosty mornings and frozen decoy lines.

So let's take a look at a few key wildfowling spots on this continent, including a few which have particularly nostalgic memories for me.

"M'gawd! Look at that!" Jim muttered to nobody in particular, as the huge swarm of pintails moved in our direction.

Moments before, a muffled roar from the south had gotten our attention, and at first we thought that the dark cloud rising from a field a mile or so away was a flock of geese. But as they came nearer it became apparent that they were ducks ... and then pintails. Four of us—Jim Rikhoff and Bill Steinkraus, two buddies of mine, plus guide John Tyler and myself—were lying in a cold, wind-swept field of rice stubble in southeast Texas, near the town of Altair, hunting a "white spread." We were dressed completely in white, including hood, and lay amid several hundred white rag "decoys" which were scattered over several acres of the field.

"John, it looks like they're headin' for the spread," I said and fumbled under my parka for a duck call. "Let's try to break a few of them outta the flock."

"Be tough with a big bunch like that." John pulled his hood down around his ears. "But get down and we'll see. Just don't move."

As the huge flock milled its way downwind past us, several hundred yards out, John showered down with a long highball call. I picked it up at the low end of the highball with a strident comeback of my own, and we alternated the invitations while peering over the rice stubble.

Neither John nor I really expected results, and for long seconds that seemed to be exactly what we wouldn't get. But when the ducks swung below our spread, and the strong wind carried the sound of the calls to them, one hen peeled from the mass and began to circle back.

"Looks good," I grunted between calls as three more pintails joined the hen—and then another pair followed suit. The mini-flock of half a dozen birds turned directly into the wind and began to bore down on a landing course for our rags, and all of us snuggled a bit deeper into our white suits.

Then it happened! The whole damn flock suddenly wheeled back and overtook the six, and now the entire massive bunch of ducks beat its way slowly into the teeth of the wind. Three hundred yards . . . two hundred . . . one-fifty . . .

"M'gawd!" Jim whispered again.

"What a sight!" Bill echoed.

Now John and I had stopped calling. The birds were committed, but it seemed to take them forever to fly those last few yards. On and on they came, etched forever in my memory against that gray, leaden sky . . . one hundred yards . . . seventy-five yards . . . fifty yards . . . forty . . . thirty . . .

Then the world turned to pintails. Eight thousand ducks tried to light on top of us, and John finally broke the spell with "Get 'em!"

My two buddies had both hunted extensively throughout the world and knew how to handle a shotgun. John Tyler is a professional duck and goose hunting guide whose dad, Marvin Tyler, originated white-spread hunting for waterfowl. I, too, can admit to having popped a few caps and killed a few birds in a quarter-century of duck hunting.

When the mass confusion was over, and the eight thousand pintails—maybe five thousand, maybe ten—were rapidly disappearing in the distance, our four shotguns were empty. And there were two—only two—pintail drakes lying dead among the rags.

The problem had been too many pintails. What a marvelous experience!

Altair and Eagle Lake, which bills itself as the "Goose Hunting Capital of the World," are headquarters for hunting geese and ducks over white spreads. They are about 80 miles west of Houston. This area is a prime wildfowling hotspot. Now let's look at some others.

Waterfowling hotspots dot the entire Atlantic Seaboard from Maine to North Carolina. Their hunting fortunes have fluctuated over the years, as duck and goose populations ebbed and flowed with changing habitat conditions.

Merrymeeting Bay, a shallow freshwater bay in south-central Maine, is perhaps the most famous name among water-fowlers in New England.

Black ducks, mallards, blue-winged teal, green-winged teal, pintails (not abundant), both greater and lesser scaup and ring-necked ducks are the key species on Merrymeeting. Goose shooting is currently not as good as in past years. Neither is the duck shooting, for that matter, but the bay still provides a lot of gunning.

Although a great amount of gunning is done from blinds, one of the traditional methods on Merrymeeting is using the sneak boat, and it was on Merrymeeting that I had my first taste of sneakboating. The technique is simple. The gunner lies in the bow of the boat and the guide in the stern, both on their backs with feet pointed toward the bow, and the guide sculls the craft within range of resting ducks or geese.

My first experience was interesting, but I am forced to say that early October might be a better time for this than was late November. Despite prodigious quantities of down clothing, I almost froze.

Scull boating for ducks has something in common with shooting over a white spread. In both you lie flat on your back until the command to shoot, and then you struggle to some sort of shooting position.

Key duck-hunting spots moving on down the Atlantic Coast include Barnegat Bay, New Jersey; the Eastern Shore of Maryland; Chesapeake Bay, between Maryland and Virginia; and Currituck Sound, North Carolina.

All of these areas, plus Merrymeeting and all of the other excellent, but lesser-known, shooting areas along the Atlantic, suffered from the same damaging ecological change about forty years ago. Vast stands of eelgrass were present in them all, and were tremendously important to waterfowl. Roots, leaves and seeds of eelgrass—all were eaten by many species of waterfowl.

Eelgrass suddenly disappeared in 1931 and 1932, victim of a plant disease. Not only was a prime food source for waterfowl gone (it was the primary food of the American brant), but the now-denuded bay bottoms were badly eroded in many areas.

The eelgrass has now returned in many of the old areas, although not all, and most of them still provide fine duck and/or goose shooting. However, the digging of canals and the subsequent draining of marshes has eliminated much waterfowl habitat along the Atlantic, and pollution has taken its toll.

Canada-goose hunting on the Eastern Shore of Maryland is excellent, with many of the birds which formerly migrated down to Lake Mattamuskeet now being short-stopped here. This is also the center of the wintering area for the greater snow goose and the whistling swan. Some forty to sixty thousand of each species winter on the tidal bays and marshes from New Jersey to North Carolina. No hunting is permitted for either.

The coastal areas of South Carolina and Georgia, and the Savannah River swamp which lies between the two states, afford fine duck shooting in certain areas. So does the Gulf Coast section of Florida just south of Homosassa Springs.

Florida has a special niche in my memory of duck hunting, since it was in the marshes south of Lake Okeechobee that I made my very first duck hunt. That first shot ever, with a 20-gauge Ithaca double, was a clean kill on a big male canvasback. It was some time before I told anyone the truth of the incident—that I was shooting at the lead duck and killed the third one in line.

Those marshes are gone, drained and placed in production of crops. But Lake Okeechobee itself still provides good shooting, with ring-necked ducks the principal fare and the Florida mallard the frosting.

Marshes! The coastal marshes of Louisiana have no equal, since they stretch from the Mississippi border to the Texas line and range from 40 to 75 miles in width. Their productivity has suffered from drainage, saltwater intrusion and pol-

Marshes are meant for ducks and geese. This one is in Louisiana, but it could be in Texas, Utah or Canada. This hunter is setting out newspaper decoys for geese.

lution, but they are still one of the superlative duck-hunting areas of the nation.

These marshes edge over into Texas for a short distance, and there offer the same quality gunning.

Catahoula Lake, in central Louisiana, has been called one of the most important wintering spots in the Mississippi Flyway. A 30,000-acre natural lake which produces enormous quantities of duck foods, it provides a tremendous amount of duck shooting for the public. The "right" water level is the key to whether that shooting is superb, fair or poor.

Stuttgart, Arkansas, is the center of an area which has provided superb mallard shooting for years, and it still does. Here is flooded timber shooting at its best, plus excellent ricefield gunning.

The bottomlands of the Illinois Valley were once a paradise for ducks and geese, and portions of the Illinois River continue to furnish fine shooting. Cairo, Illinois, because of the Horseshoe Lake Refuge, has become a concentration point for Canada geese, and consequently for goose hunting.

Two other refuges in the Mississippi Flyway have developed into enormous concentration spots for Canada geese, and with Horseshoe hold most of the honkers in the flyway during the fall and winter. They are Swan Lake National Wildlife Refuge (and the nearby Fountain Grove Management Area) in north-central Missouri, and the Horicon National Wildlife Refuge in Wisconsin.

Excellent goose shooting is the rule around all three places.

The Lake Erie marshes of Michigan and Ohio are traditionally fine duck-shooting areas. So are Saginaw Bay and Lake St. Clair in Michigan, and the St. Clair marshes on the Canadian side of the border.

The fine duck-shooting spots of Minnesota are too numerous to mention, but it is significant that one of them is the Minnesota River bottoms almost within sight of the twin metropolis of Minneapolis–St. Paul. With Bob Erickson and Sevie Peterson I gunned a pass there in the fall of 1972, and

Minnesota is one of the great duck hunting states, averaging about a million birds harvested each year. This is the bottomland along the Minnesota River almost within sight of Minneapolis, and it is prime waterfowl habitat.

although it was too early for most migrants we had a fine shoot.

The first duck I killed there, interestingly enough, was with steel shot. Bob Erickson is Director of Sales for Federal Cartridge Corporation, and wanted me to try some of their experimental loads. (I might add that I shot a limit with the steel shot that day, including a clean kill of a mallard at a measured 65 yards, but found the performance of the loads a bit erratic.)

Being the mother lode of most of the ducks which funnel down the flyways, the Canadian provinces of Manitoba, Saskatchewan and Alberta would be expected to afford excellent duck-hunting opportunities, and they do. One area worthy of particular mention is that around Lake Manitoba.

North Dakota and South Dakota have excellent duck and goose hunting. North Dakota, in fact, usually has the highest average kill per hunter in the nation.

The Eagle Lake–Altair area of southeast Texas has already been mentioned, but deserves mention again. Shooting these fields of rice stubble over a white spread is a unique kind of hunt, in that it is commonplace to have a mixed bag of Canada geese, white-fronted geese (specklebellies), blue and snow geese and ducks, predominantly pintails.

The goose-shooting future of this area is uncertain. Up-flyway refuges, largely in Missouri and Kansas, are beginning to shortstop blue and snow geese. Food and protection are holding more and more birds later and later, with some over-wintering there, and some knowledgeable waterfowl men believe that it's only a matter of time until the migration of blues and snows—and perhaps Canadas and white-fronts—to Texas ends.

Such a development would parallel the shortstopping of the Canada geese in the Mississippi Flyway which has ended shooting for these birds in Arkansas and Louisiana.

The Laguna Madre of Texas and Mexico, a vast shallow-water bay, is headquarters for the redhead. As many as 80 percent of the continental population of redheads often winters here. These areas also winter large numbers of scaup.

Northeast along the Texas coast, from Galveston Bay to the Louisiana border, lie some half a million acres of fine waterfowl marsh which is flanked by an equal expanse of ricefields. The combination provides excellent duck and goose shooting, with pintails and snow geese predominating.

Colorado, our highest state, offers some of the finest mallard shooting in the nation. Best of all is the San Luis Valley in south-central Colorado.

The state of Washington didn't cut much of a figure with duck and goose hunters a few decades back, except for the

Some marshes are wetter than others, making them more suitable for ducks than for geese. Here a pirogue trail slices through such a marsh.

great brant shooting along the coast, but have things changed! It could well be that the most consistent, high-quality mallard shooting in the nation is now to be found in east-central Washington.

A half-million acres of irrigated farmland, which came into being between 1950 and 1960, is the key to the superb gunning there. During that period the wintering mallard population for that area rose from 200,000 to more than 700,000.

The entire drainages of the Columbia and Snake rivers in Washington, Oregon and Idaho now provide similar fine

Cactus and ducks aren't usually associated with each other, but in many western locations they go nicely together. In states where water is scarce—this is in Arizona—ducks must make use of what they have.

shooting opportunities. Within this complex, mallards increased from half a million in 1950 to almost two million in 1961.

The marshes along the eastern shore of the Great Salt Lake in Utah have provided super shooting for decades, and they continue to be excellent. The Bear River National Wildlife Refuge is the pivotal point here, with excellent waterfowl habitat and a program of managed hunts. Canada-goose hunting is very good.

California leads the nation in the total number of ducks harvested by hunters each year, with a kill of over three million birds in 1970 and only a few less the following year. Best area of all is the flatland of the Sacramento–San Joaquin River drainage basin, where there are some fine marshes and several hundred thousand acres of ricefields.

Other important hunting spots in California are the Klamath Basin in northeastern California and the Salton Sea area in the south. San Francisco Bay was a prime gunning place for canvasback.

Mexico winters several million ducks and geese each year, in addition to playing temporary host to many more which are enroute to points farther south. Most of the hunting south of our border is done by hunters from the United States, and they enjoy superb shooting.

The area from Obregon to Culiacan, along the eastern shore of the Gulf of California, is one of the most consistent good shooting stretches. The grain fields, lagoons and marshes attract both ducks and geese in numbers, and quite a number of hunters.

Other key hunting areas of Mexico include the Laguna Madre south of Matamoros, and for geese the fields of grain southwest of that city; the lagoons around Tampico and Veracruz; and the lagoons along the northwest coast of Yucatan.

Ah, Yucatan! It was there, while hunting out of the Club de Patos several years ago, that I got the word from my guide.

In a mixture of Spanish, English and sign language he told me, as the expression goes, how the cow ate the cabbage.

With Mary and me on the trip were Duncan Barnes of Winchester Adventures, and Nelson Bryant, Outdoor Editor of the New York *Times*. We had arrived at the club, which is near the village of Sisal on the coast northwest of Merida, in the early evening. After a leisurely and excellent dinner, and a session of readying our guns and gear for the morrow, we retired to the bar to rap about hunts of the past and plans for the future.

A toast or two was raised, and then our host was gently reminding us that with only two hours remaining before our "wake-up" call to go hunting, it might be best if we slept a bit. We slept as quickly as possible, but I freely confess that I have been more alert than when our Mayan guide pushpoled Mary and me behind a fringe of mangroves at dawn that morning.

It was late February, and blue-winged teal made up the bulk of the duck population left in the lagoons. The teal were plentiful and swift, and they poured over the stands of mangroves and past our decoys with an elusiveness beyond my ability to cope. I shot and shot, and I sure didn't connect very often.

Mary, though normally a fair to good duck shot, had an incredible morning. Almost every time she pulled the trigger of the 20-gauge over and under, a teal hit the water.

After two hours of this the Mayan summed it all up. *"Señor"*—he pointed to me—"Bang! Bang!" And he completed the action by flapping his arms (wings) with a "you missed me" expression.

"Más la señora"—he grinned at Mary—"Bang! Bang! *Muerto!"* He closed his eyes and dropped his head to indicate that another duck had bit the dust, then broke into a belly-laugh in which he was joined by—Mrs. Gresham. Had I known the way out of that mangrove maze, and had I not

Far to the south, on the Yucatan Peninsula of Mexico, hunters have excellent gunning for teal, pintails, baldpate and other species. Best hunting is in the lagoons which flank the northwest shoreline of Yucatan south of Sisal.

had so much time invested in training Mary (how to shoot?), I might have left that swamp alone.

Where does it happen? Almost throughout North America. I've sampled only a handful of the great and interesting gunning areas of the continent in the past quarter of a century, and I plan to try some more in the next decade or two. Nobody can ever get around to trying all of them, but I can't think of a more worthwhile goal.

Chapter 5

How It Happens

HARDLY DARING TO breathe, I forced myself to remain immobile, pressed against the trunk of a pinoak. From beneath the brim of my cap I could see, almost feel, the mallards loafing past directly overhead at treetop height—less than 40 yards—gun range.

Unless you've experienced the sound, you can't imagine it. The soft whisper of many wings—more than a hundred ducks in this flock—occasionally accented by a sharp flap or two as a duck accelerated or maneuvered to avoid a collision. The low, far-reaching chuckle, not a feed call, which is almost continuous in an airborne flock of large size, punctuated by the periodic greeting of a hen and the reedy lisp of a drake.

"Steady! Not yet!" Roy Wood whispered the warning

across the ten feet separating us, as we stood knee-deep in the backwaters of the Forked Deer bottoms of western Tennessee. "They'll be back."

As the tail end of the great flock moved away, Roy began to slosh the calm water into ripples with one foot as he leaned against the oak and sent a strident come-back appeal out through the timber from his duck call. I added some sloshing of my own, and wondered again if we hadn't blown the ball game by not shooting. It was, after all, the fourth pass for the mallards, but on each succeeding one they were lower and the diameter of the circle was smaller.

But Roy had called it! This time, at his call, the flock broke sharply eastward, downwind into the south, and began to beat its way back toward us. When they were still a hundred yards out we quit kicking the water, freezing against the trees, as Roy's calls switched to the excited, short greeting mixed with a feed call. Then he stopped even that as the first echelon moved overhead.

The mass of mallards just hung there, almost motionless in the strong north wind, since they knew that this was the center of the ripples from feeding ducks down below. Then a Suzie made her decision. With a *"quaaack . . . quaack . . . quaack . . . quack"* she suddenly sideslipped and fluttered down through the timber, and that triggered the rest into following suit.

With shivers floating up and down my spine I watched that huge flock slip, slide, dive and twist its way down through the branches of the trees, dropping to the water on all sides of us. With dozens already down and more on the way, Roy finally gave the word: *"Now! Get 'em!"*

To gain gun-swinging room I took a step away from the tree trunk, and won't soon forget the expression on the drake which was swimming around 20 feet away. But then all was confusion, as the mallards roaring upward vied for airspace with those still landing in an incredible symphony of color, sound and movement.

Out of the blur there came into sharp focus an unusual bird—dark, almost black—a black duck. I nursed the muzzle of my 20-gauge Model 12 just past the outstretched bill and touched it off, only then realizing that the bird was still dropping, not climbing. I stayed with him as he reversed directions and, this time, centered him with the pattern. Swinging right, I drifted past a hen, then crumpled a greenhead.

Roy stuffed shells into his gun, checked to make sure he had no cripples, then grinned across at me. "Worth waiting for?"

"Fantastic!"

I am tremendously fond of hunting, of almost any variety, but gunning for waterfowl is my favorite. As far as methods for hunting ducks and geese are concerned, I think there are only three varieties: good, better and best. In short, I like all of them.

Wading the flooded timber

If I were pressed into a corner for one and only one favorite method, however, it would probably be timber shooting for mallards. Wading flooded hardwood bottomlands in hip boots or waders, utilizing a bare tree trunk for a "blind," and attracting ducks by calling and by sloshing the water has an attraction all its own. In no other form of gunning can the hunter put himself more into the bird's element.

The *pièce de résistance,* in timber shooting, is to make those birds commit themselves to land, to funnel down through the trees to where you are. If the ducks are skittish, or if there is too much competition in the area from other hunters or from live ducks on the water nearby, then it's frequently advisable to shoot whenever they're in range.

On many occasions I've decided to let them make one

Timber shooting is popularly associated with Arkansas but practiced in many other states as well. Hunters wearing hip boots or waders stand in shallow water, using a tree trunk as a "blind," and try to call mallards down through the trees. These three hunters began without decoys but now have four, improvised from their first kills.

more swing, only to have a better (luckier) caller a few hundred yards away take them out of my pattern and put them into his.

One big reason for waiting until they start down through the timber is to make sure they're in range. After watching a flock circle several times, with the trigger finger getting itchier by the circle, it is easy to underestimate range. More crippling is the result.

Stuttgart, Arkansas, is headquarters for this kind of duck shooting. The practice began in the overflow bottomlands of the rivers, which still furnish some gunning, but now many

In timber shooting it often helps to kick the water, creating ripples which simulate feeding ducks. Hunter on the left, caught away from the protection of a tree trunk, has wisely frozen into immobility.

duck clubs dike sections of timber and flood it to perfect depth during the hunting season.

Many of these clubs have artificial reservoirs which they never gun, to act as sanctuaries which hold a body of ducks in the area. The mallards, and some other species, trade back and forth to the timber, where they feed on acorns, and to nearby ricefields.

Wading the timber isn't the most comfortable method of shooting ducks, and that's particularly true when it is necessary to break ice getting to the shooting area. But insulated hip boots and waders make even those conditions bearable, which means delightful if enough ducks are flying.

Some hunters nail a board between two trees to serve as a seat in a favorite area, which eases the strain of standing when no ducks are moving. Many clubs have gone a step farther by building pit blinds out in the timber, often clearing an opening in front of the blind for decoys.

Although Arkansas is the leader in this kind of shooting, it is practiced in backwater situations all along the Mississippi Flyway from Illinois to the Gulf, and in similar situations along the Atlantic Flyway. The battue areas along the Mississippi River have provided some spectacular timber shooting, often in stands of willow rather than oak.

Blind and decoys

The most traditional and widespread method of hunting ducks and geese is from a blind of some kind, with the birds lured to the area by decoys. Mouth-blown calls are used in connection with the decoys in many instances, but in most of them the birds come despite the calls, not because of them. (There'll be more about this in Chapter 9.)

Being accustomed to the blind's type and location can mean a great deal to the hunter's success or lack of it. I learned that the hard way on a hunt for Canada geese in the Louisiana marshes.

I was hunting with a giant of a man named R. J. Stine on his land southwest of Lake Charles. We shot from a pit sunk in a natural knoll in the marsh, which had been left brush-covered while the surrounding area was drained and planted to winter wheat. R. J. gave me the left side of the box, my favorite, but perhaps his ideas were other than charitable.

When the first flock began to work, responding first to R. J.'s excellent calling and then to the decoys set in the wheat out front, my host cautioned me to keep down. Each time

The "classic" form of duck shooting—if there is such a thing—is gunning from a blind constructed out in a lake or pond. This one is a floating blind, but those in shallow water are often built on stakes driven into the lake bottom.

I tried to peek through the brush around the pit, to orient myself and the geese, he repeated the warning.

"Keep down! Keep down! I'll watch 'em . . . I'll tell you when!"

So I remained seated on the bench in the pit, head down, listening to the flock of Canadas get nearer and nearer. Finally when it seemed as if they were coming in the pit with us, R. J. said, "Let's get 'em!"

With the command, however, I felt the pressure of a ham of a hand on my shoulder. R. J.'s three hundred pounds unyieldingly rooted me to the bench while he stood there and killed two geese, shooting with one hand. When the flock was safely in the distance he lifted his hand and asked, "Why didn't you shoot?"

The Stine land is in the Gum Cove section of Louisiana, south of Vinton, and was the heart of superb Canada-goose

Goose hunting may be done from elaborate pits around the Illinois and Missouri refuge-shooting ground concentrations, from pass-shooting blinds on the Eastern Shore of Maryland, or from a marsh blind such as this one. Only the mud buggy makes it possible to hunt some remote areas.

shooting before the up-flyway refuges and shooting grounds shortstopped the birds. It was there that Elton Bordelon taught me a trick I wouldn't have believed.

Elton worked for a rice company in Orange, Texas, but hunted with R. J. and helped him guide his guests. One morning he had Mary and me in tow and he called a flock of a dozen or so into our pattern. But almost within range the birds slid off to one side to light in the wheat 100 yards away.

Boom! The sound of Elton's gun going off lifted Mary and me from our seats, but he cautioned us to stay down. He had

Hunting geese over a white spread—a scattering of white rags which serve as decoys—is a unique brand of gunning practiced in Texas. No blind is required. The hunters dress themselves completely in white and simply lie down in the rice stubble among the white rags. It is so effective that geese will frequently alight near the hunters. Ducks and other wildfowl decoy to a white spread equally well.

deliberately shot into the air, spooking the geese, and he immediately began calling again.

Elton calls geese using only his mouth, and his rendition of the nasal two-note call of the Canada is the best imitation I've ever heard. This time he called that flock of spooked geese back around and over our decoys, where we killed two of them to round out our limits.

"They don't know where the shot came from," Elton explained in answer to my puzzled query. "I've worked that time and again. They don't always come back, but your odds are good."

Pass shooting

Even when hunting from a blind using decoys, you'll get many pass-shooting opportunities. Ducks or geese will fly by within range, either by chance or lured on that course by the decoys, although they have no intention of decoying.

But pass shooting by itself is a popular and effective method of hunting waterfowl in many parts of the country. One of the best examples—if "best" is the right term to use—is the firing lines which surround goose concentration areas.

Such areas as Horseshoe Lake, Swan Lake and Horicon provide a rest area and protection for the birds, and a certain amount of food. When that food is exhausted, the birds range from the refuge each day (or night) to forage in the surrounding fields.

It is when they leave the refuge early each morning that gunners outside the refuge boundaries get a crack at them. Geese quickly are conditioned to seek altitude when they leave the refuge, placing most of them far out of gun range of the firing-line shooters. But there are always stragglers which fly low enough, and there always seems to be gunners who try

Pass shooting is a favorite form of duck gunning and goose shooting in many areas. This simple blind is on a pass in the Minnesota River bottoms near Minneapolis, and takes advantage of duck flights trading up and down the river.

100-yard shots. The unfortunate thing is that a tremendous amount of crippling takes place.

The firing-line fiascos aren't as numerous as they once were. Buffer zones in which shooting is prohibited have been established around some refuges, and most hunters have discovered that they are much more successful hunting from pits or blinds out in the feeding fields. Commercial hunting operations have sprung up around most of these goose refuges, and the harvest is heavy.

For several years a harvest quota has been set for the area of the Horicon Refuge in Wisconsin. When the kill reaches a certain figure, the season is closed.

Although the huge concentrations of Canada geese which have become routine at a few spots in the Mississippi Flyway have furnished good hunting in those areas, the phenomenon has several unfortunate aspects. One, perhaps the least important, is that they have eliminated gunning for these birds in the states south of these shortstopping areas.

Most pathetic, to me, is that the majestic Canada goose has changed from a wild and wary bird, king of the skies, to a ward of state and federal governmental agencies. Jammed into the concentration areas, fondly called "refuges," they have lost most of their fear of man and, consequently, most of their wariness. Each morning they figuratively line up for their handouts, their food supplements. Only the food stamps are missing.

Most serious, however, of the dangers attending the goose refuges is the potential for devastating disease. With a hundred thousand birds or more crowded into a tiny area for months, conditions are ripe for an epidemic which would decimate the population.

The first big build-ups of Canadas took the authorities by surprise, and more than two decades ago the U.S. Fish and Wildlife Service was trying to disperse the flock at Horseshoe Lake. One of our goals on the Tennessee National Wildlife Refuge, where I was assistant manager in 1950–51, was to lure geese just that 75 miles farther south from Cairo. Our success was token, and hasn't been much better in the twenty years since then.

Hunters and chambers of commerce in the areas of the concentrations don't want the birds disturbed, for understandable reasons. The huge flocks guarantee gunning, and they are a tourist attraction. Refuge managers acquire a protective attitude toward keeping "their" birds, and resist management measures which might encourage a resumption of traditional migration patterns.

Although the first build-ups were accidental, most of the subsequent ones occurred by design. Now there seems to be a very real prospect that blue and snow geese will meet the same fate as the Canadas. More and more of them have been stopping in the Midwest on their fall migration, moving on to their ancestral wintering grounds on the Texas and Louisiana coasts only very late in the winter, or not at all.

A classic pass-shooting situation exists on Remington Farms, the 3,000-acre research and demonstration area on Maryland's Eastern Shore which is owned and managed by Remington Arms Company. There a small lake plays winter host and refuge to as many as ten thousand geese and even more mallards and pintails.

The lake is never gunned, but several hundred yards away are blinds from which pass shooting is done. Each morning the geese leave the lake to feed in surrounding grain fields, and some pass low enough over the blinds to provide good shooting.

The "pass" I hunted with Bob Erickson on the Minnesota River is one he has leased for years, and is typical of many pass-shooting situations in the northern Midwest. We hunted from blinds or hides, on dry land between lakes or ponds, without decoys. The shooting was at ducks trading back and forth from lake to lake up and down the river bottom.

In the marshes of Louisiana and Texas, and elsewhere, pass shooting is sometimes more effective than hunting over decoys. This is particularly true late in the season, when blinds stick out like sore thumbs because the natural vegetation has been beaten down by weather, and when ducks are wary and gun-shy, having survived four months of gunning from Canada southward.

Ducks tend to fly a particular route, a pattern, which may change from day to day. Watch where the flight line seems to be, and position yourself along it.

On many occasions in the marshes my gunning day has been saved by moving from a blind to a pass-shooting situation. If ducks continue to skirt my spread, I don't hesitate to move. I try to select a spot where most birds have been work-

In the marshes of Louisiana and Texas mud boats like this transport hunters via ditches out into the vast area, depositing them at intervals on marsh ponds. From that point the hunters use a pirogue as their mode of transportation, either to a blind or just to the concealment of the native vegetation. This mud boat is returning after a successful morning hunt.

ing, then just squat, sit or kneel down in the marsh grass. Sometimes two or three changes of location are necessary before getting in the "right" place.

There are times, of course, when nothing works.

Jump shooting

Jump shooting, as the name implies, involves moving to within gun range of the birds, flushing them, and shooting. It takes many forms, and can be very exciting and very productive.

Walking them up is the simplest of all, and a Wyoming jump-shooting experience has to be the easiest "hunt" I've ever made. It began when Cliff Stevens said, "Sure, we can kill a few ducks if you want to."

He made it sound like buying the morning paper at the newsstand, and it proved about as certain. We drove out into the countryside from Cody until Jim stopped the pickup at a bend in the trail he had been negotiating. Uncoiling his 6-foot-7 frame from beneath the wheel, the Wyoming conservation officer said, "Get your gun!"

All I could see for miles was sagebrush and bitterbrush, but I've learned not to question a man on his home ground. After following Jim cross-country for a couple hundred yards I stopped when he did. "Crick is just ahead." He pointed with his gun barrel. "Usually some ducks in the bend right there. Best to keep kinda low from here on."

Creeping through the cactus with no water in sight wasn't exactly my idea of duck hunting, but Jim, of course, was right. In minutes we topped a slight rise and Bitter Creek was indeed right there, and from a pool in the bend sprang a dozen mallards. We killed four.

"Lookathere!" Jim pointed upstream, where several hundred more ducks had taken wing at the sound of our shots.

In parts of the country where water is limited, ducks must make do with what they've got. That means they utilize small creeks and rivers and canals and stock ponds—anything that's wet. Which means that the jump shooter has a wealth of opportunities.

While hunting deer and antelope with Henry Shipman in eastern Montana we always kept shotguns in the vehicle. Henry would know when to slow down as he approached a rise, so we could glass the ponds he knew lay beyond the hill.

If birds were on the pond, we would select a route of approach, then back the jeep back down out of sight and make our creep. The pattern in most cases was to move up the drainage from below the dam, which many times enabled us simply to walk quietly within range. Other times it was a belly-to-the-ground approach, then a one-time opportunity when the ducks flushed.

If you can walk the marsh—and in some kinds of marsh that's quite a trick—jump shooting can be good. It can also have unexpected results.

Several years ago, while filming a duck-hunting segment for *The American Sportsman* television series with Rip Torn and Burt Reynolds, we noticed that quite a few ducks were avoiding our pond to light in the Louisiana marsh a few hundred yards away. Finally Rip and Burt could stand it no longer, and decided to walk them up.

"Don't fall in a 'gator hole," was my parting advice, half facetious, as they left.

Not far from our blind they both did just that, going almost out of sight in the marsh. Rip got the worst of it, but both had to virtually undress there in the marsh to wring out their soaked clothing.

Paddling or drifting a boat within range of ducks is yet another method of jump shooting, perhaps the most popular of all. Floating downstream on a creek or river is a delightful technique. The trick here is to ease around the sharp bends on the inside, for it is in the backwater eddy around the corner that ducks most frequently are found.

Paddling a pirogue, or some other small, easily handled craft, in the thick timber of flooded reservoirs has become another favorite duck-hunting method.

Sneakboating, or drifting, is the boating-jump-shooting technique favored along the Atlantic Coast. In the former the boat is sculled toward the birds, while in the latter the boat is carried toward them by wind, current and/or tide. In both the boat is usually camouflaged with whatever seems right for the occasion, with one of the strangest being chunks of ice

Sneakboating is another classic form of wildfowling, widely practiced along the upper East Coast. This sneakboat on Merrymeeting Bay in Maine is typical. The gunner lies in the bow, and his guide (buddy)—who will scull the craft within gun range of resting ducks—lies in the rear. It is a demanding form of gunning, but often very effective.

and snow which give the craft the appearance of a mini-iceberg.

Jump-shooting ducks or geese from a boat requires particular care, since the shooting platform is usually relatively unstable. If only one man is shooting, there is little danger, but with two men gunning there is risk.

In sneakboating the stern man should swing the boat broadside if possible, which it rarely is, but to a three-quarter profile in any event. If both are to shoot, that is. In some situations, and some types of boats, it's possible for the man in the stern to stand up before shooting while the bow man remains seated.

The position of the shotguns carried in a boat is of utmost importance. The muzzles of the guns should point *above* the gunwale of the boat, with the bow man's gun pointing forward and the stern man's gun pointing to the rear. *No exceptions.* When guns are carried in this manner, an accidental discharge will go harmlessly into the air. Carrying them any other way invites a hole blown in the hull, a foot shot off, or worse.

Chapter 6

Shotguns and Shells

THERE IS NO other item of equipment used by outdoorsmen, let me be frank to admit, which has more personal appeal for me than does my shotgun. Not "a" shotgun, please note, but *my* shotgun.

I own rifles, pistols, shell buckets, jackets, boats, motors, rods, reels, lures by the thousands, binoculars, spotting scopes, vehicles, tents, camp stoves and on ad infinitum. For many of them—particularly one or two rifles which have been long and trusted companions—there are fond places in my heart. But none of them brings forth the warm glow, the pride of ownership, the delight of usage or the nostalgia of remembrance which is triggered by my shotgun.

My feeling about the scattergun is not unique. I have

countless gunning companions who have revealed such thoughts in one way or another, often in a backhanded way.

"Wouldn't own a gun if I were 'fraid of gettin' it dirty," one said between ducks one morning. Yet ten minutes later he was unconsciously brushing dirt from the receiver of his venerable pump, and he continued the hand polishing long after any dirt was gone.

There are some, it is true, who look on ole Betsy purely as a tool, a piece of steel and wood which serves a purpose. And they would no more think of calling a shotgun "ole Betsy" than they would think of parting with a favorite retriever. Nothing wrong with that attitude, naturally, but it isn't mine.

Some of my shotguns and I share a pact. We have come to an understanding, one of mutual respect and admiration. I promise to treat them well and they return the favor.

We do goof now and then. One week last season I had a terrible run of misses and fringe kills, and I could almost see the look of chagrin, even pain, on the barrel of that particular Betsy. On the other side of the coin, the safety on that particular pump gave me fits for a while last year, but then after almost three decades of faithful service . . .

Shotgun types

The most popular shotgun on the waterfowl scene today is the automatic, which is, of course, an autoloader rather than a true automatic. It has outstripped all other shotgun types for wildfowling just as it has for hunting all other kinds of game.

There are good reasons. Modern automatics have become extremely reliable in their functioning, and some or all of them offer the additional advantages of single sighting plane, fine balance and pointing qualities, three shots, and an amazing reduction in apparent recoil.

With an automatic the hunter can get off more aimed shots more quickly than he can with any other shotgun. Perhaps it's true that a slide-action repeater is *capable* of being fired faster than an automatic, the theory being that the auto action requires more time between shots than does the hand operation, but that doesn't hold true for most hunters.

It especially does not hold true for duck and goose hunters shooting from cramped blinds or pits, or shooting from awkward positions in white-spread gunning or layout shooting. The heavy layers of cold-weather clothing usually worn while hunting these birds further increases the gap between the possible and the practical.

With an automatic the shooter has merely to press the trigger three times to fire three shells. There is no shifting of hands to disturb his aim. And with the gas-operated automatics, there is little muzzle jump from recoil which might throw him off line.

There are two basic kinds of autoloading actions used in manufacturing shotguns. One is the Browning blow-back type, which uses the recoil effect itself to work the action. The other is the gas system, which uses the power of the gases created by the burning gunpowder. The Remington Model 1100 is probably the leader in the field here, although there are now many other fine autoloaders on the market. The Browning automatic itself is perhaps the foremost example of the blow-back version, but again many other brands and models utilize this principle.

Both kinds have their fervent admirers, which is quite understandable among a group as individualistic as wildfowlers.

The pump or slide-action repeater has many of the advantages of the automatic, plus a reliability almost equal to the ability of any shooter. It has the single sighting plane, large shell capacity (three shots for waterfowling), lighter weight than most autos, and good pointing characteristics.

When the end of market hunting came in this country, it is a fair bet that a great percentage of the gunners were then shooting slide-action repeaters. To take it a step farther, those pumps in most cases were Winchester Model 97's or Model 12's. Both had (have) a magazine capacity of five or six shells, giving the hunter six or seven quick shots at each flock.

It was in 1935 that a federal regulation reduced the number of shells allowed in magazine and chamber to three for waterfowl.

It has been said many times that a slide-action represents the most value for the money available to a shooter, and there is merit in the statement. Many of the pumps are relatively low in price, and are durable and efficient.

An exception to this from the standpoint of price is the Model 12 Winchester. It was discontinued as a regular production item in 1963 because it was an expensive gun to manufacture. But with a continued demand for it, plus a more affluent society programmed to accept higher prices, the Model 12 was reintroduced in three 12-gauge models in 1972 with prices beginning at $350.

All slide-actions are inherently "safer" guns than auto-loaders, simply because the pumpgunner must make a conscious effort to insert a fresh shell after he fires. Inherently, of course, guns are neither dangerous nor safe. Only the people using them can be so categorized. But the automatic does offer more opportunities for the novice or the careless to make a mistake.

For experienced slide-action shooters, when there is no problem with bulky clothing or cramped quarters, getting off the second and third shots very rapidly is no problem. Having shot pumps for almost three decades, I can testify that the "shucking" of one empty out and a fresh shell in becomes almost a reflex action.

One of the greatest feats in exhibition shooting was performed with a slide-action. Herb Parsons, who shot for Winchester, could hand-toss into the air seven clay targets simultaneously, and break all seven with individual shots from a Model 12 before they hit the ground. It's vivid testimony to just how rapidly a slide-action can be shot by an expert.

Many slide-action shooters claim another advantage for their shotguns. They say that the act of pumping the gun lets them concentrate better on subsequent shots. And with gunners who tend to touch off shots too fast, that is undoubtedly true.

Shotgunning in this country grew to maturity on single-barrels and double-barrels from England, first muzzleloaders and then the breechloaders we use today. It was around the turn of the twentieth century that slide-actions began to gain popularity, and in the next forty years they and the automatics increasingly dominated the American sporting scene.

During those decades, American manufacturers produced an array of excellent double-barreled shotguns, many of them still around and in use. Parker, Ithaca, Fox, Lefever, L. C. Smith, and Winchester with its Model 21—all are names with rich meaning in the history of waterfowling in this country.

But the pumps and the autos continued to make inroads, and after World War II the decline of the double became a plunge. Most U.S.-manufactured doubles were discontinued, either from lack of sales, or higher manufacturing costs, or a combination of the two.

In the past decade, however, there has been a strong resurgence of this kind of gun, but with a new face in the crowd. The over-and-under, a double with the barrels placed one atop the other rather than side by side, has stolen the show.

To avoid the labor squeeze of price and craftsmanship, most of these new doubles are being produced overseas—notably in Japan, Spain, Italy, Belgium and Germany. Some side-by-side doubles are now originating from this side of the water, and in 1973 Remington began U.S. production of the

Model 3200, a reintroduction of the famous Model 32 over-and-under which had been discontinued in 1942.

Key names in the double-barrel field, both conventional and over-and-under, are now Browning, Winchester, Beretta, Charles Daly, Savage, Krieghoff and Franchi. Some of the old English names are still around, notably the Purdey and the Holland & Holland, but their prices are so high that they make little splash in wildfowling in this country.

Doubles, in any form, have the advantage of giving the gunner two readily available chokes. With no need for a re-loading mechanism, or the space for it, doubles can be several inches shorter than pumps or autos of the same barrel length. They are probably the safest of all shotgun types, with the chambers in full view when the gun is broken.

The conventional double has the finest pointing quality of any form of shotgun. The side-by-side alignment of the barrels produces a balanced, streamlined instrument which is beautiful to use. In reloading, the "break" of the action is shallow, slightly more than the diameter of one barrel.

The over-and-under dominates the twin-tube scene in this country largely for two reasons: availability of better-quality over-and-unders than side-by-sides at a reasonable price; and a nation of shooters grown accustomed to a single sighting plane.

Although the over-and-under is not quite as nimble in pointing quality as the conventional double, it is still a thing of beauty. Veterans of the classic side-by-side doubles criticize the "break" of the over-and-under, which must be twice as deep to free the empty from the bottom barrel, but such a complaint would never occur to gunners moving from a pump or auto to the over-and-under.

Any double has one disadvantage in many waterfowl hunting situations. It is awkward to reload unless the barrels are either level or pointed downward; in other positions one shell will fall out while you're putting the other in.

The additional firepower of pumps and autos is no longer

Firepower isn't of supreme importance in this era of low daily bag limits, perhaps one of the factors which has stimulated the increased popularity of over-and-under doubles. Doubles, such as the 20-gauge Winchester 101 which Jim Lester is manning in the Arkansas timber, have the additional advantage of offering an instant choice of two chokes.

a valid point in making a choice of shotgun actions. Sheer numbers of birds in the bag has long since ceased to be a criterion for the success of a hunting trip, with both bag limits and public opinion mitigating against that notion.

Shotguns have personalities. Some are quick and nimble, some are ponderous and awkward, and many are somewhere in between. Of all the actions, the double in both forms is the most sprightly. More of the weight is between the gunner's hands, enabling him to get the muzzles on the target faster.

The longer sighting place and slower response of pumps and autoloaders, on the other hand, have advantages for some. For them these qualities help them to point more accurately, to be more deliberate in their shooting and to follow through after pulling the trigger.

You pays your money, as the saying goes, and takes your choice. One thing is certain. That choice is wider and better now than ever in history.

Shotgun chokes

Choke in a shotgun is a constriction in the barrel at the muzzle. Its purpose is to control the spread of the shot after it leaves the shotgun barrel.

In the days b.c. (before choke), when barrels were true cylinders from one end to the other, the effective range was short. Shot began to disperse immediately after leaving the barrel and, according to Fred Kimble, the "greatest range any shooter could expect from this shotgun was 40 yards."

Although details of choke origin are hazy, most give this Fred Kimble credit for first producing a workable choke in 1867. He was a market hunter living in Illinois, and with his new muzzleloading single-barrels, choke-bored, he could "kill at 60 or 70, and one of them at 80 yards." These were probably 9-gauge guns, which seemed to be Kimble's favorite size.

Modern choke designations are derived from a standard formula: the percentage of shot from a given load in a 30-inch circle at 40 yards. Arbitrary, but generally accepted, are the following degrees of choke: full—65–75 percent; improved-modified—60–70 percent; modified—55–65 percent; improved-cylinder (skeet #2)—45–55 percent; and cylinder (skeet #1)—35–45 percent.

From the percentages it is obvious that the customary designations are anything but precise. In theory, and in practice, a modified and an improved-cylinder barrel could be the same—at 55 percent patterning. Most barrels, with most loadings, will shoot patterns somewhere toward the middle of the designated range, but only rather extensive testing of an individual gun with a particular shell will give the true picture.

Gun barrels are peculiar critters. Most will pattern some loadings (brand, powder charge, shot size) better, frequently far better, than they will others. Most hunters make the mistake of never experimenting with their shotguns on a pattern sheet, and they should do so. In that way they can quickly determine the most effective combination for them.

Full choke has been "the" choke for duck and goose hunters down through the years, but the average gunner would be more successful with less than that. Improved-modified, which isn't generally available, or modified, which is, would result in more kills and cleaner kills.

That full choke is the ultimate for the longest range, of course, but hitting flying birds at those distances with any consistency is beyond the skill of most hunters. In addition, in most situations there is no need to attempt those extreme shots.

For the past six years I have done most of my duck shooting with a 20-gauge over-and-under bored improved cylinder and modified. The efficiency of that more open barrel at putting ducks on the water is amazing, and that broader pattern compensates to some degree for errors in gun pointing.

According to one gun and ammo manufacturer, the outer

limit of the "ideal range" for an improved-cylinder boring is 30 yards. Over decoys, a big percentage of the ducks shot would be inside that limit.

My recommendations? For the expert shot (who really needs no advice), full choke where most shots will be long-range ones, modified for general conditions, and improved-cylinder for shooting over decoys. For all others, which includes most duck and goose hunters, modified is best.

For the small gauges, the 28 and the .410, which are really tools of the expert, borings should generally be tighter. With the smaller number of shot in these little shells, the shot strings must be more confined in order to have a dense, killing pattern.

Shotgun gauges

The system of referring to shotguns by gauges started many years ago. A gun's bore size was designated by the number of round lead balls that just fit the bore it took to weigh a pound. Thus, the bore of a 12-gauge gun could accept a round ball, twelve of which weighed one pound.

The exception is the .410 gauge, which would more properly be called a .410 bore. The diameter of a .410-gauge barrel is .410 inches. By true "gauge" designation, a .410 bore would be 67½ gauge.

Federal law prohibits the shooting of waterfowl with any gun larger than a 10-gauge. Today that is academic, since few gunners now use anything bigger than a 12-gauge, which is the most popular size shotgun for all gunning in this country.

With the proper choice of shells, either 12, 16 or 20 gauge is satisfactory for most duck and goose shooting. For the average shooter with no physical handicaps, a 12-gauge gun is recommended. For the youngster, or for ladies or men who might be recoil-conscious, a 20-gauge is frequently more effective.

Keep in mind that all waterfowl are hardy birds, so use a gun which will help prevent cripples. Sportsmanship, or the lack of it, doesn't lie in the size shotgun one chooses, but in the manner in which the shooter uses it.

The 28-gauge and the .410 are strictly for the specialist, inadequate for most of us. That doesn't mean they are entirely ineffective.

"Gene, kill that snow!" The command came from Marvin Tyler one morning, while I was shooting with him over a white spread in Texas. A white-garbed figure on the fringe of our setup came alive. There was a toylike *pop-pop* from that direction, and the snow goose dutifully plunged from the ranks of the flock of specklebellies to hit the ricefield with a thud.

"There's no other hunter I'd trust to do that, to kill one goose out of a flock like that," Marvin told me later. "Gene Sentell is the best."

In that particular instance all of our party had limits of "dark geese"—specklebellies or Canadas—so only the lone snow in that flock was legal fare for us. At face value it was excellent shooting, since the goose was at least 30 yards away from Gene and probably farther, but it was more remarkable because he was shooting a .410-gauge shotgun.

Sentell, who is from Louisiana but now lives in Houston, is one of the best shots on geese I've ever seen, and I'm sure he is equally adept on other game birds. He shoots nothing but Model 42 Winchester repeaters, which are .410-gauge slide-actions.

On geese he uses No. 4 shot, and a typical .410-gauge 3-inch shell will have 92 of these pellets in its 11/16-ounce charge. Assuming a 70 percent, full-choke pattern, out at 40 yards Gene has 64 No. 4 shot to work with in that 30-inch pattern.

How does he do it? He shoots the geese in the head and neck. That's a feat seemingly beyond the skill of most gunners, but consider that the head and neck of a goose contains more vital area than does an entire mourning dove. The flaw here is that most shooters, even possessing the necessary ability, can't make themselves shoot at the head rather than the body of the goose.

At any except pointblank range, that .410 load centered on the body of a goose is a crippler, no more. Centered on the head and neck, which Gene Sentell can do, it is effective.

Larger gauges, of course, would be even more effective. The more dense the pattern at any given range, the more effective the killing efficiency. A .410 and a 10-gauge may give the same 70 percent pattern at 40 yards, but the latter is much more effective because its 70 percent contains many more shot.

Barrel lengths and stocks

I like them short!

That succinctly states my feelings about stock and barrel lengths on shotguns for waterfowl. On the latter, especially, that runs contrary to most that has been written and to the feelings of most hunters.

We can dispose of stock length very quickly. Heavy clothing and cramped blind or pit quarters, which are typical of most waterfowling shooting situations, often make it difficult to mount a standard-stocked shotgun with ease. A shorter stock will usually result in improved shooting success.

An average field gun has a length of pull of about 14 inches. That's the distance from the trigger to the center of the buttplate, and 14 inches is just about right for a man of average dimensions who is standing erect in good shooting position, wearing normal-weight clothing. In a duck or goose blind he would perform better with 13¾ inches, or 13½ inches, and in some cases on down to 13 inches.

But a little reduction goes a long way here. Even a quarter-inch is quite noticeable in the way a gun handles.

Drastic surgery is sometimes necessary. Mary, my wife, has hunted with me for more than twenty years, and it was only two years ago that I discovered that the stocks on her shotguns were too long for her. I had shortened all of them, of course, allowing for her 5-foot-2 height and arm length to match, but it wasn't enough.

At her insistence I cut the length of pull on her over-and-under back to an even 12 inches, a full 2 inches from the normal. Her shooting, already good, showed an immediate and significant improvement.

Keep in mind that shortening a stock can be overdone. Above all, remember that you can chop a stock down by degrees until you get it just right. It's a lot more difficult to add inches back on once you've cut them off.

Barrel lengths on most shotguns are either 26, 28 or 30 inches, with a few available out to 32 inches. There is no difference in the effective killing range between a 26-inch and a 32-inch barrel.

The "long barrel, long range" syndrome stems from the black-powder days. Those slow-burning powders required a longer barrel in order to develop full power for the shot charge. That is no longer the case with modern smokeless powder, hence all else being equal, a gun with a 26-inch barrel will kill a duck or goose just as far as will one with a 32-inch barrel.

I shoot better with 26-inch barrels than I do with 30-inch barrels, and I believe that most waterfowl hunters would. The reason, in my estimation, is that it makes for a "quicker" gun, a more responsive gun.

Because of the action, a pump or autoloader is some 4 to 6 inches longer than is a double with the same barrel length, so with them barrel length is especially important to handling quality of the shotgun. It is sometimes difficult, however, to get a 26-inch barrel in full choke, or even in modified.

Manufacturers, understandably bowing to the desires of most shooters, seem to have arrived at a rather fixed "choke-to-barrel-length" ratio. Cylinder and improved-cylinder—26 inches; modified—28 inches; and full choke—30 inches. With doubles it is usually 26 inches for the improved-cylinder and modified and 28 inches for the modified and full.

There are exceptions—brands where you can get a 26-inch barrel bored modified or full, and 26-inch barrels for doubles which are modified and full.

The longer sighting plane of the long barrel obviously has some advantage in trap shooting, but in waterfowl gunning I think any possible loss in that direction is more than offset by the better handling quality of a shorter barrel.

Shotgun shells

In no other aspect of shotgunning have there been so many great improvements in the recent past as with shotshells. Those we shoot today are far more efficient than any available two or three decades ago.

One of the great advantages of the new shells, as far as waterfowl gunners are concerned, is the plastic hull. Unlike the old paper hulls, plastic cases don't swell and bulge and refuse to chamber when they get wet.

From a performance standpoint, the biggest improvement has been the protection afforded the shot as it passes through the barrel. Plastic sleeves and capsules surround the shot charge inside the shell and as it moves down the barrel, falling away a short distance from the muzzle. This keeps the lead shot from being deformed by friction against the barrel, ensuring that more of them fly true to arrive at the target as programmed.

Better wads, seals, crimps, primers and powders have also

contributed to making modern shotshells marvels of efficiency.

Shot sizes for shooting ducks and geese can and do range from No. 2 to No. 7½. As a general rule of thumb, the bigger the bird the bigger the shot size which should be used. A teal which might flit through a pattern of 4's would be smothered by 7½'s. The smaller shot, on the other hand, lack the penetration needed on Canada geese unless the range is very short.

For shooting ducks over decoys, hunters who can impose self-discipline against long shots will find 7½'s ideal. Express loads are customary, but even field loads are satisfactory if the birds are decoying well. Out to 30 or 35 yards that dense pattern gives very clean kills. If you might succumb to temptation, or the situation calls for longer efforts, move down to No. 6 shot.

The most efficient shot size on mallard-size ducks at all feasible ranges, when using a 12-gauge gun, is No. 4. Tests have shown that the average gunner cripples fewer ducks with 4's than with smaller shot. The advantage decreases as you move to smaller gauges because of a decrease in pattern density.

When gunning the large Canada geese, No. 2 shot are called for. These are big birds that require a lot of killing. Only in close-range shooting over decoys should smaller shot ever be used, and even then nothing smaller than 5's is practicable.

For lesser Canada geese, white-fronts, blues and snows, No. 4 shot is just about right. For long-range shooting you might drop back to 2's, while over decoys 6's will do a good job.

But bear in mind that how your particular shotgun handles a shot size will also influence the particular load you use most of the time. Experiment to see what gives you the best, most consistent patterns.

Magnum loads have their place, but they are no substitute for getting birds within good range and centering them with the pattern. A duck or goose which *is* within good gun range, and which *is* centered with a shot pattern, will usually be cleanly killed regardless of what gauge, choke, or shot size is used.

Keep in mind that many waterfowl market hunters used rather light loads. One reason was that they were being frugal with powder and shot, but none would compromise his ability to kill ducks for the sake of that saving. They matched their loads to shooting conditions.

Years ago I had a forced experience with light loads which taught me something. A late-night call from a friend reported many ducks working the backwaters of a flooded lake, and did I want to go hunting the next morning? Naturally! Then I discovered that the only shells I had in the house for my 20-gauge Model 12, which was the only shotgun I owned at the time, were light field loads of No. 8 shot.

The next morning we selected a "blind" in the timber at the fringe of a flooded cornfield, a small patch of cultivated land far back in the timber. All we did, in fact, was to place our decoys in the open, then run the bateau beneath a leaning dead tree.

Mallards worked as if we had them on strings. Using my quail loads, I started with the variable choke set on full, but by the time we quit shooting it was at improved-cylinder. That huge pattern of 8's was simply poison at the 20-30-yard range, and I've never forgotten the experience. I don't mean to suggest that I recommend light loads of 8's for ducks, needless to say, but the fact remains that in most of our hunting situations, the capability of modern guns and shells far exceeds the ability of most shooters.

Chapter 7

How to Hit 'Em

BEING A RELIABLE shot in the field on waterfowl involves far more than mere shooting ability on moving targets. A great many gunners who have the latter skill, prove mediocre when in the duck blind or goose pit. There's quite a difference.

This chapter, consequently, deals with much more than the basic ability to hit a moving target. It concerns itself, in addition, with the techniques by which the average waterfowler can put more ducks or geese on his table.

The basic premise in wing shooting is that the gun must not be pointing at the bird when the trigger is pulled, because, as the great Adam Bogardos put it, "a flying duck doesn't stay in the same place very long." It must, instead, be pointing at a spot where the bird will be when the shot charge gets there. The shooter who neglects this elementary principle, except in the case of a bird flying directly away or directly toward him, will inevitably shoot behind the bird.

In short, you must lead a bird in order to hit it, which won't come as news to shotgunners with any experience at all. But how to arrive at the proper lead is something else again, and there are two schools of thought on this. Both have their uses.

School number one is the "sustained-lead" form of shooting. In this method you simply point the gun the prescribed distance in front of the bird, swing along in that position, and pull the trigger while maintaining your swing. In the second method, frequently called the "swinging-through" technique, the shooter swings his gun at a faster rate than the bird is traveling. As the muzzle passes the bird he pulls the trigger, maintaining his fast swing.

It's the latter method that causes same good shots to say, "I never lead a bird." The fact is that they do start their trigger pull when the gun is pointed directly at the bird, but by the time the charge leaves the barrel the muzzle has moved to give the required lead.

The swinging-through method is taught at the Holland & Holland Shooting School in London, and I had the opportunity to sample that type of instruction several years ago. In this method the gunner programs his actions, his mounting of the gun and turning of the body to follow the flight of the bird, so that the muzzle is on target the instant the gun butt hits the shoulder. At that moment the trigger is pulled. No apparent lead.

The method works. I shot it on overhead targets from a 50-foot platform and from a 100-foot platform, giving no apparent lead, yet broke the targets consistently. For this technique to work, of course, the gunner must be in a position to swing his body freely, a luxury that duck and goose hunters don't always enjoy.

Could you close your eyes and hit a target thrown from

a trap? I did, following the instruction of Rex Gage, and it was a rather revealing experience. "Watch the target leave the trap," Rex told me, "then close your eyes, mount the gun, and fire the instant the butt stock hits your shoulder."

I did exactly that, and broke the target. To prove that it was no accident, I did it again. It was a matter of the mind programming the body to swing along a predetermined path, a path calculated in a split second by that amazing computer we call a brain, and of firing the moment the gun was mounted.

The swing-through method of shooting is faster, but more waterfowlers use the sustained-lead principle. Even they, however, go to the swing-through technique occasionally, albeit unconsciously. Almost everyone has had the experience of having a bird appear suddenly, followed by the comment, "I didn't have time to aim. Just poked the gun at him and pulled the trigger." What the shooter was unconsciously doing was to swing very rapidly in the direction of the bird's flight, and pulling the trigger when he thought the gun was on the bird. The lead was automatic.

Head position

One of the most common causes of poor and inconsistent shooting on game birds is the failure of the shooter to position his head in the same place on the stock shot after shot. This is of vital importance because the head serves as a rear sight when shotgunning.

You've heard the expression, "Keep your head down." Many a trap or skeet shooter has watched a target sail unscathed into the distance because he failed to do just that. More important than simply keeping it down, however, is to keep it in the same spot each time. I have seen some excellent, consistent shots on both clay targets and game shoot with an erect head position, but they shoot like that every time.

The essential thing is that you discover what sight picture is best for you, and that you try to duplicate it each time you shoot. Only in this way can anyone develop into a consistently good game shot.

Some poor to mediocre game shots have benefitted in recent years from using one of the new optical sights which are on the market. Both versions of this sight project a bright-red or orange aiming spot which represents the center of the pattern at a prescribed distance.

This aiming dot is, in effect, a substitute for that immovable head position. It gives the gunner a mechanical aid which tells him exactly where the pattern will go, shot after shot.

One type of optical sight can be used whether the shooter closes one eye or not, but the other requires that he keep both eyes open. Using two eyes for wing shooting is recommended in all cases, since the binocular vision of two eyes is far superior in instantly estimating range, speed, angle and deflection of a moving object.

Stock fit

Because a consistent head position is so important, gun fit—and here we mean stock fit—can be quite critical. In fact, it is vital to the "instinctive" method developed by the late Robert Churchill which is taught at Holland & Holland. When I was introduced to this method the first step was to find my correct fit on a "try gun." This is a shotgun with a stock which is completely adjustable in all dimensions—length of pull, drop at comb and heel, and cast-off.

To find my correct stock dimensions, Rex Gage stood me about 30 yards from a huge pattern board on which was inscribed the outline of a flying bird, and had me shoot at it as quickly and naturally as possible: "Pull the trigger as soon as the stock hits your shoulder. Don't wait, and don't aim." Then he would adjust the stock a bit and have me try it again. Finally the pattern was centered over the "bird" and Gage was satisfied.

The dimensions which Gage found perfect for me with the Holland system were a longer length of pull and a higher comb than I normally shoot, plus a slight cast-off to the right of no more than ⅛ inch. The latter corrected for a pattern which was consistently printing on the left edge of the bird.

Bear in mind that I was standing erect and wearing normal clothing, conditions which aren't quite typical of most North American duck or goose hunting situations.

For European hunting of driven game birds, the H & H method of shooting is excellent, and very fast. Since there are situations where it is applicable to our gunning, let's examine it a bit, in Rex's words.

"Never look at the gun or barrel at all. This is a basic consideration. Notice that I don't drop my head to the gun. The head is still, and the shoulder comes to the gun, with the stock just touching the cheek.

"The body imparts the swing. I am not moving the gun, as such; I am merely turning my body. I point at the bird— *shoot!* Point at the bird—*shoot!* The first choice must always be the one; never make any correction. If you do, you upset your timing. Correct gun mounting and correct timing—this has got to be 100 percent correct."

The difference between this method and the way most of us shoot is this: We mount our gun and *then* swing with or past the bird, although we usually are swinging the gun as we bring it toward our shoulder. Rex swings with the bird, by body movement, as he mounts the gun, with the trigger being pulled the instant the gun butt touches his shoulder.

However, don't overemphasize the stock-fit business. Most normally proportioned people can shoot well with most stocks of average field dimensions if they give themselves a chance to become familiar with them. The exception, as noted elsewhere, is that a slightly shorter than normal length of pull is better for most duck and goose situations.

Practice

Becoming a good wing shot calls for practice, as much of it as you can get. Since game-bird shooting opportunities are restricted by seasons, limits and most gunners' time free for hunting, clay targets offer the solution.

It is much easier for a good shot to help a beginner (or a mediocre shot) on clays than on live game. Skeet and trap ranges are excellent for this, and all clubs have members who are able and willing to give advice. Hand traps offer even more variety.

The more you shoot, the better you'll get to know your shotgun, and until you and it become almost as one you'll never achieve that distinction of being a cut above "good" as a wingshot. The gun must be an extension of your will, doing your bidding without question.

The opposite is commonplace. Too frequently the appearance is of a shotgun dominating its owner. He points in the general direction of the target, and pulls the trigger, but it's obvious to the knowledgeable that the gunner's operation is out of control.

Practice mounting, swinging and pointing your shotgun on a regular basis and the empathy between you and it will grow. You can do this even in your home, where targets abound—doorknob, lamp, or a spot on the wall or ceiling.

A word of caution! *Each time* you pick up that shotgun, at home or in the field, open the action to make sure it is not loaded.

To get the most benefit from clay-target shooting, from a standpoint of greater field-shooting skill, do your practice shooting with shotgun at "ready" position rather than with it already mounted when you call pull. All trap shooters, and most skeet shooters, do the latter, but skill in mounting the gun after the target is "flushed" is what the wingshooter needs.

Timing your move

The ability to go into action at just the right time is a quality which separates many excellent game shots from mediocre ones. In every shooting situation there is one moment which is "best" for that particular circumstance. Shooting just a little

PHOTO BY HURLEY CAMPBELL

Correct timing of the gunner's move is one of the most important points in hitting ducks or geese. This duck is in perfect position for the shot. (Even so, if you're on the point-system bag limit you still might not shoot, since this is a hen mallard worth 90 points.)

too soon or a little too late makes a lot of difference in the results.

There is no way to describe precisely that magic moment, but all great wing shots know it when it arrives. Even so, it isn't always possible to put it all together. Even the best make mistakes, when watching a flight of circling pintails or honkers through the thick cover of a blind, in estimating distance and deflection.

"Don't move and don't call as long as they're still headed your way" is a time-honored axiom among waterfowlers. We'll delve into the calling later, but the "don't move" part has great value.

It applies almost completely to birds coming in toward decoys. The chance that they'll get in too close is nowhere near as great as the chance that they won't get near enough. Rising to shoot at such birds when they're still 40 yards out, and still approaching, is one of the great errors made by many waterfowlers. Letting them move another 10 or 15 yards would probably double the chances of success.

Forty yards is decent gun range, but consider what often happens. The hunter rises from concealment when the duck or goose is at that range, but by the time he gets the shot off the bird has flared to 43 or 45 yards. Now it's getting marginal, both for the killing efficiency of the gun and for the ability of the hunter to center the bird with the pattern. That first bird falls crippled, perhaps to be lost. The hunter's second and third shots are at birds 50 yards away and farther, and prospects for a clean kill or a downed bird of any description are dim.

Consider the alternative: letting the flock come on in to 25 or 30 yards before shooting. With any luck, all birds will be within optimum range for two or three shots.

Waterfowl are most vulnerable to a shot charge when facing in your direction, and lead is easiest to determine when they're approaching. Next on the preferred list of situations is the right-angle, crossing shot. Worst of all is the going-away position; the bird is least vulnerable to shot and leads are most difficult to determine.

Try to time your shooting to take advantage of the best conditions. A bird which is quartering away from you is much more difficult to hit than one quartering toward you, so act

A shot at these geese over a Texas white spread would be sky-busting at its worst. Before you can hit and kill ducks or geese they must be in range, which is probably closer than you think. At 60 yards, for instance, perfect shots on mallards with a full-choked 12-gauge would kill only 64 percent of the time. Even at 50 yards perfect shots would miss or cripple 15 out of every 100 ducks.

Timing your shooting move is particularly important when the shooting must be done from an awkward position, such as this almost-prone attitude typical of white-spread gunning. Practice the possibilities before the game appears.

accordingly. Whenever possible, I try to get off my first shot before the birds are spooked at all, which often can be done if you ease into shooting position instead of making an abrupt move.

A knowledge of how any particular species of waterfowl reacts to gunfire is extremely helpful in proper timing. Diving ducks making a run over your spread will normally just pour it on and bore on through when you rise to begin shooting. A flock of teal making the same type of approach, on the other hand, will usually flare and climb. Program your move accordingly.

Skip the candy bird

In any flight of decoying ducks or geese, there will be one or two birds which we call "candy birds." They are by all odds the easiest shots, the candy shots, and they jump out at hunters. They're the birds responsible for "doubling," when both hunters in a blind shoot the same duck or goose.

If you want to kill more than one bird from that flock, ignore that candy bird with your first shot. Size up the flight as best you can before it's over the decoys, and as you rise to shoot pick the second-easiest bird—or the third-easiest—on your side of the flock. They'll be birds which are a little farther away than the lead candy bird, or candy birds, yet they'll still be within excellent gun range.

Always work your way *forward* in the flock, not backward. After you've killed that second- and/or third-best bird, that flaring candy bird will still be within good range. Of course, modern bag limits are such, in most places, that multiple kills from each flock are anachronistic. When shooting is good, in fact, we frequently will intentionally shoot only one bird from each flight that comes within range, and in these circumstances you may as well pick the easiest shot you've got.

PHOTO BY HURLEY CAMPBELL

Again, this is perfect timing, with the gunner having allowed both drake pintails to move into ideal position before making his move to take the lead duck. The tendency of most gunners is to succumb to the urge to shoot the first duck as soon as it is in range, which puts those coming along behind at extreme range.

There are times, however, when one or two flocks will be your only opportunity all day long. At such times your ability to discipline yourself and ignore the candy shot can be the difference between one or two birds and a limit.

The hot shots

"Man, I'm told you I don' believe what I see. We almost to d' blin' and I fin'e Mister Guy got one box of shells. Hmmmmp! I know I done los' my bet."

There is more involved in bagging wild ducks than marksmanship, and the ability to coordinate your shooting with your gunning partner is an important aspect. You must communicate, so that both of you make your moves at the same time. It's fundamental that each gunner shoots his side of the flock or pair.

Noah Schexnider, a tall, ramrod-straight Frenchman who grew up in the marshes of Louisiana, was describing for me a trip on which he guided Guy Ward. The bet was a daily one with the other guides at that club, and the winner was the first man back at the clubhouse with his twenty-five-duck limit.

For Noah the day had begun badly, the night before, when Guy instructed him that he wouldn't be going out until eight the next morning, which would be long after the other guests were shooting. Then, having pushpoled the pirogue almost to the blind, he noticed the lone box of shells at Guy Ward's side.

"De sun was way up when we got in de blin'," Noah continued, "and right quick I calls a big bunch o' French ducks in. Mister Guy lets 'em light, den stans up and scares 'em away. He don' shoot one time. Then he says, 'Now, let's kill some ducks, Noah.' And did he kill some duck!"

In less than an hour Guy Ward killed twenty-five mallards and pintails, had one shell left, and never shot a duck on the water. He was back at the clubhouse with his limit long before anybody else, so Noah won the pot for that day.

Ward, who grew up on Reelfoot Lake in Tennessee, where his dad operated a lodge, had ample opportunity to hone his shooting skills just before and after the turn of the century. Great flights of ducks poured down the Mississippi River basin, and the shooting on Reelfoot and along the nearby river was fabulous.

His skill first became known to the rest of the nation on June 2, 1906, when the twenty-year-old country boy hoisted his gun, packed his bag and burst out of obscurity to win the first North American Amateur Trapshooting Championship. It was the beginning of a long, illustrious career, during which he served as an exhibition shooter for more than one arms and ammo manufacturer.

Guy Ward was just one of many superb waterfowl wing

shots developed in this country during that era. The skill of the real hot shots, on ducks or geese, is a world apart from the normal good gunner.

George Doescher, another Louisianian, market-hunted the marshes from 1900 until 1913, shooting a 16-gauge Model 97 pump. "We usually killed two ducks with the first shot," George told me. "Flying, of course, since they're harder to kill on the water."

It was normal for Doescher to kill five ducks from a flock, and his contemporaries acknowledge that he often killed seven. He did not, needless to say, take the candy shots first.

Market hunters, and those who shot for sport, developed similar shooting skill all along the Mississippi Flyway and along the East Coast. Game was abundant, limits were non-existent or very high, and the ability to shoot was a respected skill among the entire population.

The development of excellent wing shots did not end with market hunting, and the past few decades have produced some remarkable game shots. One of them was the late Herb Parsons, and before him Nash Buckingham, both—like Guy Ward—from Tennessee. I have hunted with men from coast to coast who have that uncommon touch with the scattergun when it is applied to ducks and geese. They will never be recognized for their skill, as were the likes of Bogardus, Kimble, Carver, Ward, Buckingham or Parsons, for ours is another time, another era—an era in which the killing of large numbers of birds is not only unfashionable, but illegal.

Paint your pattern in the sky

The shot pattern from a shotgun has depth as well as width and height, the latter two generally conforming to a circle. A short shot string, with most shot arriving at the target about the same time, is highly desirable, but a true one-plane pattern seems out of reach.

I find it helpful to keep that fact in mind when wingshooting, and try to think of my shotgun as a paint brush. My goal is to "paint" a splotch of shot pattern up there in the sky that my bird will run into.

Keep reminding yourself that most misses in wing shooting are the result of too little lead rather than too much. When in doubt, leave a little more air between your muzzle and the outstretched neck of duck or goose. If you are a bit too far in front, the length of your shot string may compensate for your error; if you are behind, you miss with the entire string.

Another prime reason for concentrating on enough lead is that by doing so you're working on the vital areas of the birds. It's those shots centered toward the stern section of waterfowl which are cripplers.

Choke

Choke has been discussed in an earlier chapter, but any discourse on how to be a better wing shot would be incomplete without something on this. Waterfowlers in this country have a fixation on the full-choked shotgun, and for most that is a severe handicap.

With reference to choke, one very apt saying goes, "It lengthens your reach, but may lighten your bag." Gough Thomas put it well in his book, *Shotguns and Cartridges:* "The best degree of choke for filling the game bag is always the least degree consistent with the requirements of the class of sport concerned."

There are exceptional barrels, but it is a characteristic of most full chokes that the patterns they throw are very dense in the middle and sparse toward the edge. Patterns generally improve, from a standpoint of pellet distribution, as the degree of choke decreases.

At long range, therefore, the killing portion of that full-choke pattern is quite small, usually beyond the ability of most gunners to center it on a flying bird. Closer in, at the modest ranges where most birds are killed (and more missed), that full-choke pattern is even smaller.

It is my considered opinion that most hunters in most duck and goose shooting situations would kill far more birds, more cleanly, with a modified choke than with a full. In many, many instances the improvement would be even more marked if the gunner went to improved-cylinder.

Less choke means bigger, more efficient patterns, which in turn means more clean kills at normal ranges.

Kill that cripple

Tens of thousands of ducks and geese are lost each year because hunters hesitate before shooting a crippled bird. Don't wait! If the bird shows any appreciable signs of life after he hits the water, shoot him again.

Waterfowl are extremely hardy birds, and can often recover sufficiently to escape after being hard hit. When they first fall they are generally within range of a finishing shot, but any delay may permit them to drift or swim out of range.

Ducks on the water don't offer much to shoot at, and can be difficult to kill. A good practice is to carry along loads of fine shot—7½'s or 8's are good—for use on cripples.

Make friends with your shotgun

To be an expert wing shot you must make friends with your shotgun. It must become a part of you. You must caress and cuddle that hunk of wood and steel, for there is more than just a bit of tart among the ingredients which separate the good shots (and perhaps the good guns, too) from the poor.

You must acquire and then maintain confidence, both in your shotgun and in your wing-shooting ability. Only when you get to the point where you *expect* the bird to fold when you pull the trigger can it happen with any consistency.

Chapter 8

Blinds and Boats

THERE IS NOTHING very complicated about duck and goose blinds. Waterfowl, except where they have been semi-domesticated by refuges, are wary birds which have a natural or acquired fear of man. That being the case, they won't venture within gun range if they can help it.

To cope with this the hunter conceals or camouflages himself by a wide variety of techniques which range from the prosaic to the ingenious. Let's examine some of them.

The early waterfowl hunters simply hid in whatever natural cover was available, and many still do just that. Where the situation lends itself to this, it can be the most effective of all.

Marsh vegetation—grasses, rosseau cane, cattails, bullwhip

—frequently is used as a "blind," by hunters both on foot and in boats. Freezing motionless against the trunk of a tree in flooded timber, or along the edge of a lake or stream, serves the same purpose. Concealment behind a rock on the shore-line can get the job done.

The white-spread hunters use a camouflage technique

A typical stake blind, similar to those found throughout the country, constructed on pilings driven into the lake bottom. Most gunners camouflage these blinds with native vegetation but it isn't unusual to get good shooting from those which are left bare, the birds becoming accustomed to a fixture in their habitat.

without a blind. They dress completely in white, hood and all, and lie amid several hundred white rag "decoys," blending into the spread so effectively that geese often light within feet of them.

But most hunters try to improve on nature, constructing a blind which is either built with materials native to the area, or covered with them to blend in with the surroundings. The blind is a place of concealment, where the hunter can stand, sit, squat, kneel or lie, and may be primitive or luxurious.

The phone rings.

"Yeah?"

"There's a big bunch of mallards headin' down the lake in your direction. We broke 'em off and they made a couple swings around our blind, but we couldn't get 'em on down. Looks like new ducks."

"Okay, thanks. We're just cooking some hamburgers, but I'll wake John and have him get outside to watch. Call you back later."

Those blinds aren't exactly primitive. They're on Black Bayou Lake in northern Louisiana, and are virtual homes on stilts out among the cypress trees. Most are carpeted, have cots and cooking facilities, and are connected with each other by a private telephone system. Outside the enclosed room is a shooting deck completely encircling the blind, which itself is completely surrounded by several hundred decoys.

They are mini-versions of the big clubhouse blinds, some underground, which once were sprinkled along the eastern coastline. In those comfortable rooms club members lounged, playing cards, eating or sleeping, moving to the shooting deck via an underground passageway only when ducks or geese were in.

A man I know struggles each fall to move his houseboat back into South Carolina's Savannah River swamp. There he camouflages the whole thing, puts out decoys, and shoots from the top deck. Inside: all the comforts of home, including color television.

But those are the exceptions. The usual duck or goose blind is an affair which conceals the gunner but offers little protection from the weather.

"Are ya cold, honey?" I noticed that my wife had stopped shivering, was indeed quite still, but that the sleet and snow continued to build up on her rain suit.

"No, not *cold.*" Mary still didn't move. "I'm frozen! You didn't have to go to all this trouble for my benefit—rain, sleet, snow and snowballs. Any one of them would have been sufficient."

Since dawn we had been in an open pit blind on the shore of a small Utah lake. The weather had been moderate for openers, but then we got all the variety Mary spoke of, in quantity. It was a real whistling blue norther that moved through, and we weren't prepared for it. I was as cold as she was but refused to admit it.

Our blind faced south over the lake, and behind us the terrain sloped upward for a few hundred yards. The frigid north wind, laden with rain, sleet and snow, hugged the contour of that slope with a passion, right into our blind, and seemed to blow completely through us.

Compounding our misery was the fact that there were no ducks or geese flying. We would have returned to the comfort of civilization but had no wheels, and no desire to walk the five miles. Just before the truck came to pick us up a small flock of Canada geese swept over the slope, past our blind on my side, and when they suddenly appeared, I killed one in a conditioned-reflex move. But then something stayed my trigger finger, and I didn't even shoot the other barrel.

It just seemed that the weather was miserable enough for geese without having somebody shooting at them.

Blinds can be separated into three general classes. First are those built entirely above the level of either ground or water. Second are those which are entirely below the level of ground or water. And third are those in between, with part of the blind down below and part protruding up above.

The sinkbox, a blind on the water which is sunk to the surface, is not legal. Often called a battery, these were extremely popular along the East Coast, and were tremendously effective. In a sinkbox the gunner was completely below the level of the water until he rose to shoot. The sinkbox was surrounded by a big spread of decoys, with a pickup boat stationed downwind to collect the dead ducks as they drifted.

Just how effective a battery was is indicated by the report that one market hunter on Chesapeake Bay killed 506 ducks in one day shooting from one.

Pit blinds, the land-based equivalent of the sinkbox, are both effective and legal. They can be a simple hole dug down into a sandbar or cornfield, or a blind constructed of wood or prefabricated of steel or plastic and sunk into the ground.

This comfortable shooting pit, made of steel, is sunk into a rice-field levee. The top of the pit is on rollers which let it glide back out of the way at a gentle shove.

One of the best pit setups I've ever shot from belongs to a friend of mine who is a duck guide near DeWitt, Arkansas. Lewis Rush sank a 10-foot-long, rectangular pit made of steel down into one of his ricefield levees. Immediately adjacent, but separate, he placed another small pit from which he calls. The big one can accommodate four to six gunners.

Both pits have tops which are on rollers. When Lewis says "Let's get 'em," a push on the top sends it rolling back out of the way. The pits don't protrude from the levee more than

Though the "blind" used in most timber shooting is nothing more than a tree trunk, this Arkansas duck club has built a shooting pit out in their flooded area. Such pits are built of concrete or steel when the area is dry, as it is most of the year; the water is pumped in just before the hunting season begins.

a foot or so, and during the summer Lewis lets the grass grow up around them. He floods the ricefield immediately around the pits just before the duck season opens, and sets out several hundred decoys in that 6-inch-deep water.

It's a super setup. The pits are dry, and can be warmed by portable heaters. They offer perfect concealment from approaching ducks, and almost instant availability of room to shoot. This is typical of the better pit-shooting arrangements throughout the continent, with minor variations to suit individual situations.

Blinds which are half-submerged or half-buried are most adaptable to marsh gunning, and to hilly shores surrounding lakes or streams or bays. In the marsh it is often difficult to bury a pit completely, since the water underground tends to

The typical marsh blind is little more than a rectangular enclosure camouflaged with native grasses and reeds. Though very effective when they blend in with the surroundings, such blinds stand out conspicuously late in the season when the native vegetation dies down, and ducks and geese frequently become "blind-shy."

"float" the blind right out. Such pits can be anchored securely in a half-buried position, which lowers the blind silhouette.

With just a minimum of digging, the slope of a hill can be used as the back of a blind, with a bench seat for the shooter carved in the hillside. Only out front need any actual construction be done.

Above-ground or above-water blinds can be simple or elaborate. Those on water can be floating, or permanent. They can be designed so that the boat itself is used as the shooting platform, or so that the gunners climb from their boat into the blind. They can be so small that they won't conceal a boat, in which case the shooters must have means of transportation to and from their shooting station, plus someone to retrieve their birds.

Blind variations, obviously, are endless. The simplest "ready-made" pit blind I've ever used was a 55-gallon drum sunk into the ground. It wasn't very comfortable, since I couldn't fold my long legs up enough to get out of sight when the geese appeared. But it worked. Two 55-gallon drums split and fastened together side by side, another pit which I've experienced, make a much better blind.

The most elaborate store-bought pit is a one-man affair manufactured in California. Built from watertight fiberglass, it has a seat which adjusts for height and rotates 360 degrees; a ten-foot utility shelf for shells, calls, thermos, binoculars and camera; a gun rest and an underseat heater; and a lid which can be used for concealment or to keep rain or varmints out.

In many cases the boat itself has served as a blind, and the sneak boats and layout boats of the East Coast are perfect examples. Camouflaged with material which was appropriate to the time and place, they either allowed the shooter to approach within gun range (sometimes), or so adequately concealed the gunner that the ducks would decoy to it.

The layout boat is just what the name implies. It is a shallow-draft boat, usually for one man, and is camouflaged completely with local vegetation. In use it is pulled ashore

This commercially available fiberglass blind puts the gunners below ground except when they rise to shoot. Note the difference in appearance made by sprinkling native vegetation on the blind cover on the right. The bare fiberglass on the left is conspicuous to our eyes, and more so to ducks and geese.

into a patch of that vegetation, and the gunner lies down in the boat. When birds come within range, either decoying or passing, he sits up to shoot.

Using the boat itself for a blind is still popular in many areas, with the ingenuity of hunters at devising means of camouflage knowing no bounds. Camouflage netting draped over the boat is simple, and often very effective. White sheets do the job on a boat pulled ashore on a snow-covered bank.

Collapsible blinds can be useful. It is simple to weave native reeds or rushes into lengths of chicken wire which can be rolled for storage and transporting. Then, once the boat is beached or anchored, you simply fasten those blind sections along the sides and ends of your boat. Brackets fastened at

This wildfowler has simply worked his boat into the reeds surrounding a pond. This makes one of the most effective "blinds" of all, but it's possible only if the native vegetation is high and dense enough to provide concealment.

appropriate intervals along the side of the boat, and steel or aluminum rods on the ends of the blind sections, make this a simple and quick chore.

Such portable blinds can be used on shore or in the marsh, of course, and are often the solution to temporary shooting situations.

Two blind arrangements from which I gun regularly indicate different techniques of using the boat as a shooting platform. In one the blind is floating; in the other, fixed.

Jim Lester, a long-time shooting companion, hunts from a square-stern, "sport model" aluminum canoe. At the blind location of his choice in the marsh he first builds a blind frame which closely follows the outline of the canoe. Two vertical posts (2x4's) are driven into the ground at each end and two more amidships, one on each side. Then 1x4 strips—two on each side—are nailed to the posts, curved to fit the boat outline. To this frame he fastens chicken wire, and weaves into it native rosseau cane as camouflage. It makes an excellent blind.

One end must be left wide enough to permit entrance of the canoe, with the 2x4's on that end spaced just far enough apart to handle the beam of the boat. Jim lets the 1x4's extend about two feet past the posts on that end, however, which conceals the stern of the boat from view.

But isn't a canoe pretty unstable to shoot from? Not after Jim gets through. He uses a C-clamp on each side to fasten the canoe gunwales to the center 2x4 posts, which changes the platform from shaky to stable.

Frank and Bill Murphy also shoot from their boat, but the waters of Catahoula Lake where they hunt can vary from a foot to 10 feet deep. Their answer is a floating blind.

Their blind floats on two styrofoam logs which run down either side parallel to the boat. The superstructure of the blind is much like Jim's canoe blind, but the whole affair is wider to accommodate the bigger boat needed for the open water. For better concealment in the wider blind, the sides are tilted inward at the top, leaving just enough room for a gunner to stand and shoot.

The Murphys use a different technique to make their boat steady for shooting. They build runners across the blind, underwater, so that they must pull their aluminum john boat up on them when they enter the blind. The boat is almost floating, but not quite. It is actually resting on the runners attached to the blind, which makes it very steady. To make it even more stable, add the C-clamps.

Some duck boats have rings at each end, along the gunwales, through which poles can be pushed down into the mud to hold the boat steady.

I've shot from very simple blinds on land, in Minnesota and in Maryland, which were adequate. They were nothing but a head-high, rectangular frame which was covered with marsh vegetation or cornstalks, depending upon the location. We just stood inside, peeking over the top, and waited for birds to pass within range.

I've seen some very effective blinds built up in trees, some of them so high the shooting angle on decoying birds would be downward. Most of the very high ones are single-man affairs, with steps nailed to the tree trunk for access.

But I do remember one bigger blind, quite high, which keeps haunting me.

"Let 'em come! Let 'em come! Don't call any more!"

Leary Taylor cautioned me against going into action too soon, as we watched the big flock of mallards swing into the wind and begin the long descent toward our decoys. They had circled three times before committing themselves to our spread.

From our blind built 20 feet up in the triangle formed by the trunks of three cypress trees, we had watched several such flocks circle on that frigid, gray day. None, nary a single one, came within gun range. Time was running out, and we had not fired a shot. So we had made a pact that we would make the most of any flock which did make a mistake—we would let them light before making our move.

Automatics at ready, we peered over the edge of the blind as the birds came nearer and nearer, led by a hen which quacked periodic greetings to the decoys. Only once did the flock falter from line, and a quick, short *"Quaaack . . . quaack . . . quack . . . quack!"* on my call jerked them back on the track.

"Let 'em get all the way down," I agreed as the birds slid from our sight, below the edge of our blind. We listened for the sound of ducks hitting the water down below . . . and listened . . . and listened. In vain!

"M'gawd, look at that!" Leary spun me around. We watched in minor shock as some thirty big mallards disappeared over the timber behind us. They had been all ready to land amid our decoys, but something changed their minds at the last moment.

The whole flock flew directly *beneath* our blind, and when we picked up the blocks and headed for home we still hadn't fired a shot.

Ever hear of a stump blind? It's designed, of course, to resemble a tree stump, an item which is a familiar sight to ducks and geese in many areas.

The circular affairs can be made from aluminum, fiberglass, lightweight galvanized metal or even canvas stretched on a frame. Most are made in two sections for portability, and painted and/or camouflaged appropriately.

A top helps. Cut a circular top from plywood, about the same size as the blind. Suspend it over the blind on a pole which you can push into the ground, using a pipe and pipe-flange connection on the top so it will swivel. When the birds are close, just swing the top aside and come up shooting.

Camouflage, for waterfowl blinds, is a peculiar thing. I have gunned from stake blinds which were laboriously treated to match the surroundings, and with success. But, on the other hand, I have had great shooting from stake blinds which were not camouflaged at all.

Where a blind is permanent, ducks grow accustomed to it; they will feed beneath and around a stake blind built of bare wood. When a new one is constructed, however, it may be quite a while before waterfowl give it their confidence.

One great value of natural camouflage around the blind opening is that it helps conceal any movements made by the hunters.

Boats for duck and goose hunting

Boats for waterfowl hunting will obviously vary greatly depending upon shooting conditions. A houseboat doesn't readily come to mind when such craft are discussed, but proves practical for that Savannah River hunter I mentioned.

However, there are two boat designs which have become classics for waterfowl hunting, and probably the most famous of all is the sneakbox, or sneakboat, frequently called the Barnegat Bay sneakbox since there is where it rose to fame.

Samuel Bonnell, in Eugene Connett's book *Duck Shooting Along the Atlantic Tidewater,* gives an excellent description of the Barnegat Bay sneakbox: "The original sneakbox is a broad-beamed, shallow boat, varying in length from 12 to 14 feet, with a beam of approximately 4 feet. It is round-bottomed, with a slightly rounded deck rising a little above the waterline, and carries a draft of roughly 6 inches. A hatch is amidships with a cover that can be locked in place for stowing duffle."

Variations of this boat are still in use all along the Eastern Shore, and indeed throughout the nation. Some are a bit longer, some have a flat bottom, some a square stern while others are pointed at both ends. Common to most is an open cockpit substantially smaller than the dimensions of the boat itself, the craft being decked in front, rear and sides.

Most boats which are called "duck boats" around the country had their origin in the Barnegat Bay sneakbox.

The other classic design is the pirogue. Originally a hollowed-out log, most pirogues are now made from marine plywood, fiberglass or aluminum. It's probable that this boat originated in the marshes of Louisiana, where it is still used extensively, but it is now popular in many areas where an extremely shallow-draft boat is needed.

The pirogue is just that. The better ones will float on a heavy dew, and can be paddled or pushpoled with ease. Many are rather sensitive. As one Cajun guide remarked as he poled me through the marsh, "If ya chew tobacca, m'fran', don' switch it from one side t' de other less you shifts yo weight."

In most situations the actual shooting isn't done from the

The traditional duck boat has overtones of a kayak, pirogue, and Barnegat Bay sneak boat, the particular emphasis depending upon location. The Louisiana version leans toward the pirogue, as might be expected.

pirogue. It's simply the conveyance which takes you across the shallow marsh ponds to your blind.

Shorter, wider, one-man pirogues made of fiberglass have become popular duck boats in some areas of late. Some even have small electric motors for propulsion. They're frequently used for jump shooting in thickly timbered reservoirs, but are equally adaptable for decoy or pass shooting.

The companion craft to the pirogue in Louisiana is the mud boat. It is a flat-bottomed, shallow-draft, narrow-beamed boat which normally utilizes an automobile engine for power. It's an inboard, with the shaft and propeller in a recess which helps protect them from damage. Some are very fast, and most will almost literally run on wet mud—hence, mud boat.

Pirogues are used in much of South America and in Mexico, as well as in the southern portion of the United States. This Mayan duck guide in Yucatan zips along in a diminutive craft which is tailored to the size of its operator.

In use they transport hunters, from two to a dozen depending upon the size of the boat, down the canals and ditches of the vast marshes. The mud boat will stop at intervals, discharging a pair of hunters (or hunter and guide) at each spot, where a pirogue waits as the final leg of transportation to the blind.

A pre-dawn ride in a mud boat at 40 miles an hour along a winding mud-boat ditch, barely as wide as the boat and flanked with marsh vegetation, is an experience worth the price of admission. The unmuffled roar of the engine, which glows red-hot in the darkness, sends its shock wave of sound along that particular corridor of the marsh, disturbing its residents from tranquillity. Ducks, geese, herons, egrets, ibis and coots spring, struggle or lumber into startled flight, only to glide back to a landing when the boat passes.

A guide hunches over the engine, which is located amidships for balance, with one hand on the tiller and the other on the throttle. With or without benefit of spotlight he peers ahead, knowing that if he misses a twist in the trail the mud boat will plunge to a high-and-dry location out in the marsh.

Hunters making the run for the first time will peer ahead with the guide—for the first few minutes. Then they'll join the old-timers who are hunkered down in the mud boat, facing the stern, fighting to survive a wind-chill factor which defies down jackets.

Conversation over the unbridled roar of the engine, of course, is impossible.

Broader-beamed semi-V's, usually constructed of aluminum, are widely used throughout the nation by waterfowl hunters on the bigger lakes. Winter weather often means rough water, and boats such as these are necessary for the safety of heavily clad, hip-booted hunters. Permanent blinds on these lakes, whether floating or stationary, usually include a boat stall alongside or beneath to accommodate the bigger boats.

Over the past quarter-century the aluminum bateau has

Fast mud boats—some run 40 miles per hour or more—transport duck and goose hunters via mud-boat trails into remote portions of the marsh. A pre-dawn mud-boat ride at speed down a trail which isn't always as wide as the boat is an unforgettable experience.

The flat-bottomed bateau or john boat, square at both ends, is one of the most useful types of craft for hunting waterfowl if water conditions aren't rough. This one is built of marine plywood, but most are of aluminum.

been produced and sold in greater numbers than any other boat. Most are used for fishing, but a tremendous number also make their mark with duck and goose hunters.

Often called a "john boat," the bateau is narrow and flat-bottomed, and squared off at both ends. In its average configuration, nominally a 14-footer with a 4-foot beam and 16-inch sides, it is not a rough-water boat, but bigger versions are available which extend its usefulness greatly.

A rather recent addition to the array of waterfowl-hunting boats is the "bass boat," which, during the 1960's, became the best-selling fiberglass boat in the country. The qualities

It isn't a boat, but the ungainly marsh buggy is an efficient vehicle for transport-ing waterfowl hunters into remote marsh areas. These ingenious vehicles can cover terrain which is impassable for boats or for man on foot, "swimming" any deep water encountered along the way.

which make it an excellent fishing boat have many advantages to the duck hunter.

Like the bateau, a bass boat is generally narrow for its length, with a 56-inch beam about normal for a 15-footer. But the bass boat is built of fiberglass and has a cathedral hull, which gives it tremendous stability. A big man can stand on one gunwale, for instance, with no danger of capsizing, and this stability is a decided asset for a shooting boat.

Two other specialized boats which play a significant role in waterfowl hunting, but on a more localized basis, are the canoe and the airboat. The canoe is most popular for use in hunting in the northern half of the United States east of the Rockies, while the airboat is largely useful only in some areas of Louisiana and Florida.

The mud buggy isn't a boat, but this ungainly, awesome creature has transported thousands of gunners to their rendezvous with great duck and goose hunting. They clank, grind, puff and spin their way across miles of swamp and marsh which would not brook passage by either conventional boat or airboat. Over much of it a hunter couldn't walk, even if he cared to try.

Chapter 9

Calls and Calling

"A DUCK CALL in the hands of the unskilled is one of conservation's greatest assets," Nash Buckingham wrote in his great little book *De Shootinest Gent'man*. Nash Buckingham should know. He was born in Memphis, Tennessee, and shot the great flights of ducks which poured down the Mississippi River Basin at the turn of the century. Not only was Buckingham acknowledged to be one of the finest exponents of long-range shooting on waterfowl, with his favorite 12-gauge Burt Becker magnum, he was also renowned as a master with the duck call.

The above line in Buckingham's book is from a chapter which he entitled "The Neglected Duck Call." Nash would be the first to admit that the duck call is no longer neglected, although in a great many cases the gunner would have a heavier bag if he didn't even own such a gadget.

"If you're going to hunt with me, you'll have to leave that whistle in your pocket." Elemore Morgan pointed to my prized duck call, which I was fondling. "That's the only rule I have in my marshes, except that you shoot the ducks on your side of the flocks."

Elemore Morgan was a most exceptional person. The epitome of a New Orleans gentleman, possessed of all the sensitivity and savoir-faire typical of the aristocracy of the Crescent City, he was also a marvelous hunter and a spectacular wing shot on waterfowl.

For Morgan the prohibition against calling was right. He gunned the fine marshes southeast of New Orleans, selecting good-sized ponds where his modest spread would be ample attraction to passing flocks. It was seldom that Elemore Morgan didn't kill his share of the ducks.

Superb naturalist and taxidermist that he was, Morgan could also make a mistake in identification.

"Just a bunch of teal," Morgan muttered through a mouthful of sandwich as he twisted to check the flock I had spotted off his end of the blind. We had pulled his canoe into a fringe of mangroves and marsh grass just protruding into Lake Borgne, with two dozen decoys on either side. It was midmorning on a bluebird day, and with half a limit lying in the boat, we were taking a coffee-and-sandwich break.

"*Mallards,*" Morgan shouted, glancing up over my shoulder.

That "flock of teal" had made a big swing around the pond and settled into the wind, and as they hung over the decoys we saw that they were indeed mallards.

Teal, we had agreed, would not be shot except as a last resort. It was mallards we wanted. Coffee, coffee cups and sandwiches went in all directions as Morgan and I scrambled for guns and went into action. Our first hurried shots missed ducks at pointblank range. The second shots from our pumps centered on the same unlucky Suzie and she crumpled decisively. Shaken by the realization that we had doubled, we each missed our third shot.

As we sat there surveying the catastrophe, Elemore gave that wry grin and concluded, "I don't think one duck with six shots is too many."

Despite the obvious success of the no-calling technique which Elemore Morgan utilized, and which would probably increase the success of most waterfowlers, there is no denying the fact that the man who never calls a duck or goose is missing one of waterfowling's great thrills. I shall never forget the first time I talked a hen mallard into leaving the water and flying 200 yards through the flooded timber to my waiting gun. The astronauts who landed on the moon could not have felt any greater sense of achievement.

Most of the elements of effective calling of both ducks and geese can be itemized, catalogued and dissected. But when you've done all of that, there still remains an intangible factor which defies explanation. Proof of this pudding is graphically illustrated by the many times in which I've had other "less skilled" callers take birds away from me.

Another intangible we should keep in mind is that all waterfowl do not react the same way. There are days or parts of days when calling, no matter how good, is completely ineffective. The ducks or the geese just ignore it.

That's a bit difficult for many people to understand, until they consider that ducks, like people, are individuals. People don't always react the same to certain situations; neither do ducks and geese.

Calls or decoys?

A favorite topic for duck-blind discussion is the age-old ques-

tion: Which is more important—a duck call or decoys? Assuming that the caller is adequate, I would answer the question like this: On big open waters, if I had to make a choice
between decoys or calls, I would choose the decoys. On small
potholes or flooded timber, on the other hand, the call would
get the nod. The ideal situation, of course, is to have a good
spread of decoys *and* a man who can call ducks or geese.

Calling contests

Duck- and goose-calling contests are popular in many sections

*Contest calling is quite different from calling ducks or geese, but it is an
interesting and enjoyable aspect of the sport. Stuttgart, Arkansas, is host to
the "world series" of duck calling each December, and it was there that this
young lady was doing her best for the judges.*

of the country, with Stuttgart, Arkansas, being headquarters for the duck callers and Iowa getting the nod for the goose callers. Calling contests are interesting both from a participant and a spectator point of view.

The duck-calling world series is held the first Saturday in December in Stuttgart, and it's a combination of a week of fun and frolic and duck hunting. For several days preceding the main event there are elimination contests, street dances, barbecues and other affairs designed to provide the visiting duck hunter with pleasurable activity after his morning hunt. Throughout this period the streets of the small south Arkansas town ring with the sounds of duck calls, as thousands of people wander the streets, duck calls around their necks, advertising their skills or practicing their highball.

Although flocks of ducks high overhead during the Stuttgart festival are not an uncommon sight, the contest calling is done for the benefit of judges, not ducks. Contestants are identified only by number and perform out of sight of the judges, a situation which led to one of the best stories to emanate from the world series. One year, so the story goes, a live hen mallard was slipped into the finals and performed beautifully. But when the judges' decisions were announced the mallard had finished in seventh place. It could happen.

"Man, he sure can call judges, but he sure can't call ducks," is a common saying among the fraternity. So is "he can really pull those ducks in, but he couldn't have a chance in a contest."

Contest calling is a game in itself, and this particularly applies to duck-calling contests. Contestants must render a rather stylized repertoire of calls designed to display their ability to the judges. It typically opens with a series of extremely long, drawn-out highballs, the call designed to get the attention of passing ducks. The caller pretends that the ducks are responding, and moves through the successive calling sequences to bring them into gun range.

Highball—greeting—comeback—feed   call—comeback—single

quack—feed call. That, with variations, is what the judges expect, and the best contest callers are artists in action. With style and feeling they run down the scale with never a bobble, and some of them win contests. And just like the skeet or trap champs who can't hit birds, some of these tournament winners aren't particularly good at calling ducks.

What makes the difference? The key ingredient is that the

A duck guide works his magic on a circling flock of mallards, eyes alert to the reaction of the birds to each note. Blowing a duck call is like playing a musical instrument, for that's exactly what it is. The cupped hand around the end of the call mutes and directs the sound as needed.

good hunter can read the ducks he's working, and adjust his calling to the particular situation on that day. He is instantly aware of the reaction of the ducks to his pleas.

Of course, some expert tournament callers, national winners, are also superb duck callers and hunters. Dud Faulk, a call manufacturer who grew up in the marshes of Louisiana, is such a man. He has hunted ducks and geese all his life, and knows waterfowl by heart, but he has also won national titles in both duck- and goose-calling contests. There are many others like Dud, but there are also many who can call judges beautifully but birds poorly.

The development of duck calls and duck calling in this country apparently began in Illinois. A Frenchman named Glodo gets most credit for the kind of call which evolved from that area, although he may just have brought it to perfection rather than originated it.

In a twist of history reminiscent of the "Kentucky" rifle, which originated in Pennsylvania, the Illinois "Glodo-type" call is now known as an Arkansas call. It's one of two major types which account for most call sales throughout the nation.

The other is the Louisiana call, often referred to as a marsh call or Cajun call.

Despite opinions to the contrary, a duck call is nothing but a musical instrument. On it the hunter must be able to "play" the notes in a duck's vocabulary, and as with any other musical instrument, perfection requires a great deal of practice.

The parts of this instrument are the barrel and the keg, the outer, visible parts of the call. The barrel acts as a funnel for the sound, while the keg, which fits into the barrel, holds the inner parts. Those inner parts are the trough, which is the sound chamber; the reed; and the wedge, which holds the reed in place over the trough.

There are two primary differences between the Arkansas and Louisiana calls. In the former (Glodo-type), the keg and trough is usually a one-piece affair, while in the Louisiana call

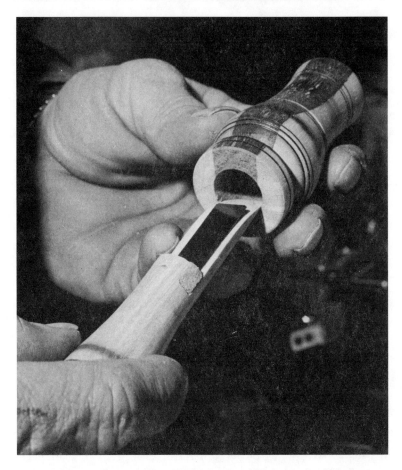

An Arkansas call goes together. The big end is called the barrel, which directs the sound. The little end is called the keg, which in the case of the Arkansas call such as this is integral with the trough, the sound chamber over which the reed lies. The wedge holds the reed in place.

they are separate. This marsh call was first made with native cane, because that was the material locally available, and the nature of cane makes it impractical to construct keg and trough in one piece.

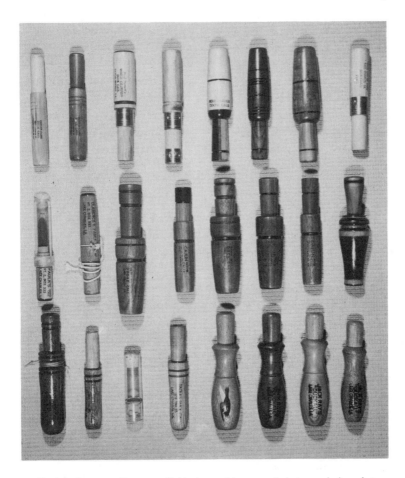

Duck and goose calls are available in a wide array of shapes and sizes, but the two basic types of duck call are the Cajun (marsh) call and the Arkansas (Glodo) call. Top right in this photograph is an example of the Cajun call, while the middle right call is a classic Arkansas type.

The other major difference is the size of the hole in the end of the keg—much bigger in the Louisiana call. The result is a loud, raucous, far-reaching call which is perfect for the marsh country in Louisiana. The small hole in the Arkansas call, on the other hand, makes for a more subdued, muted tone which is right for the woods shooting of Arkansas, Illinois and other states.

Famed exhibition shooter Guy Ward was the owner of an original Glodo call, and several years ago I prevailed upon him to tell me what he knew of its maker. As Guy remembered him, Glodo was a small white-haired Frenchman, who showed up on Reelfoot Lake around 1900 or a little later. He wasn't sure where Glodo came from, but had an idea it was from Illinois.

Market hunter George Doescher added credence to the belief that the duck call did originate in Illinois. Since he did his market hunting in the marshes of Louisiana, I asked George (in 1954) about the Cajun call. That was a mistake.

"Cajun call!" George snorted. "When I started market hunting the Cajuns didn't know what a duck call was. That was in 1900 and I was sixteen years old. I patterned my call after those of some hunters from Illinois."

Most duck calling is based on the mallard call, which is

A finished Arkansas call, left, and the ingredients which go into it, plus the die used for making the sound chamber.

effective for almost all species of puddle ducks. There are variations from species to species, of course—thin, reedy quack of the pintail to the high-pitched, short series of the teal—and many of the better callers learn to imitate these species when it is appropriate. It is equally effective most of the time, however, simply to stick with the mallard call.

Learning to call

The best way to learn the true sounds of ducks is to listen to the ducks themselves. The best way to learn how to call ducks is from a skilled caller who has the patience and will take the time to teach you. An excellent aid in learning how to call, with or without either of the above two situations, is one of the good duck-calling records which are available.

In the winter of 1950–51, when I was assistant manager on the Tennessee Wildlife Refuge, I had an unusual opportunity to observe and listen to ducks. For days on end I watched and listened to some seventy-five thousand mallards and pintails feeding in a flooded cornfield, and from my hiding place nearby I would listen to the individual ducks and try to imitate them on my call.

One of the things I learned from that session is that not even all ducks are proficient callers. Strange as it seemed at the time, and it still does, there were some ducks which were rank amateurs at the art of calling.

But a key point which should be made is that the worst calls did not alarm nearby ducks. I can only conclude that the quality of the call, and especially the timing of the call, was authentic enough to be natural, even if the notes left something to be desired.

Take that one point to heart! The timing of the notes in a call may well be the most important part of it.

If you are serious about learning to call ducks, take advantage of every means at your disposal. As often as possible, get

Proof of the call is in the blowing. Harold Rush, of Crockett's Bluff, Arkansas, gives the sound test to the instrument he has just crafted. As with any musical instrument, reed adjustment can be made to suit individual preference.

your instructor to demonstrate for you his techniques, and try to match them note for note on your call. When your wife or neighbor complains, take your instructor off to some nearby lake or stream, or to some remote spot on a lonely road outside town. Practice, under cover of darkness if need be, until you can accurately predict exactly what sound you will get each time you blow the call.

The call of most diving ducks, such as scaup, ring-neck, redhead and canvasback, is a short *"brrr, brrr, brrr"* and is quite easy to imitate. Without decoys it has little value, but it can be useful in drawing the attention of a passing flock to your spread.

A pintail whistle can be extremely effective at decoying pintails, widgeon and sometimes other puddle ducks as well. Both the pintail and the widgeon make whistling sounds, although the sounds of the two differ, and their notes are rather easy to imitate.

Several manufacturers have pintail whistles on the market, and all are effective. Some hunters can do a good job just by whistling.

Calling geese

It's usually easier to learn to call geese than to call ducks. The calls themselves are easier to master, and almost all goose hunting is done over decoys. Many hunters simply use the goose call to get the attention of the flock and then rely on the decoys to get them on in.

The sounds of the various species of geese differ greatly. The deep, resonant, two-noted honk of the Canada has little in common with the high-pitched gabble of blues and snows, nor with the almost indescribable voice of the specklebelly. Mixed flocks containing more than one kind of goose are not uncommon, but for best results, try to match your calling to the predominant species.

Calling ducks by mouth is extremely difficult, but there are quite a few hunters who can call geese without the aid of a mechanical call. Easiest to lure in this fashion are the blues and snows; the Canadas are next; and the white-fronted geese are most difficult to imitate. Here Johnny Gaspard does his thing on a flock of Canada geese.

Gearing your calling to the reaction of the birds is very important with geese. If the flock is headed your way, don't do anything to rock the boat. When flying geese are decoying to live birds on the ground, their talk becomes more excited as they approach. In this respect they're like mallards, only more so, and the caller should take note of this and call accordingly.

When to stop calling

There are two distinct schools of thought as to just when a hunter should quit calling a flock of birds. The first, subscribed to by a majority of the gunners who call at all, is to shut it off as soon as the ducks or geese are headed toward the caller. "As long as they're coming, don't call" is their motto.

The other, smaller school holds that calling should continue until the call is dropped and the gun raised to shoot.

There is no one "right" method with respect to this little controversy, and the most successful waterfowlers are flexible enough to use the best of both schools. Although they have their preference, they adapt from day to day if their particular technique isn't getting results.

If you're only a mediocre caller, discretion is the better part of valor. Call only as much as you have to, since the more you call the greater chance you have of blowing a false note and spooking the flock.

The key point is to watch the birds closely as they circle or approach. If they begin to stray from the pattern which will bring them to your decoys, immediately use your call to lure them back into line.

The advantage of continuous calling, for those who are proficient and where ducks or geese are responding, is that the flock is never permitted to "think" about wandering from a journey to your blind. It's led by that constant string of notes down to a rendevouz with your decoys.

Duck and geese can become call-shy! They can reach the stage, caused by weeks or months of heavy gunning, when even the finest brand of calling will turn them off. Under those conditions the best place for your call is in your pocket.

Browsing about calls

A duck call is a very personal thing with most hunters. Not just any call can be blown by just any man. The type of call, its physical dimensions and the way it's tuned play substantial roles in determining which call is right for whom.

A caller will blow with a certain force of wind, and the tuning and the reed of the call must be geared to that force. If the reed is too stiff for the wind volume, the sound won't be there. If too soft it'll be overpowered, to stick, break and jam.

Try many calls, including individual specimens of the same brand and model, until you find one which seems to suit you. Then stick with it.

Duck or goose calls won't perform properly if sand, dirt, tobacco or twigs get in to interfere with the reed. Care for your call accordingly. Like most hunters, I find it best to drape mine around my neck by a cord. As a safety precaution, to keep from losing the keg if the call comes apart, tie your string to both barrel and keg. Commercial lanyards are available which have a spring-loaded noose for each end of the call.

Two callers better than one

Under most conditions two good callers working a flock of birds from the same blind will be much more effective than one. They complement each other, with the notes of one picking up where the other leaves off, parlaying a medley which can be irresistible.

Would you believe *five* callers?

Years ago, while hunting knee-deep in the flooded backwaters of a Tennessee river bottom, I had the frustrating experience of having flock after flock of mallards called away from me to another group of hunters several hundred yards away. I could get the ducks to make a swing or two around me, especially if they originally came from my direction, but then the symphony of sound from the other calls took its toll.

Time after time the finale of the act would find me watching a huge flock flit through the bare hardwoods in the distance, then settle down into the trees. A moment of silence, then a fusillade which would have done credit to any tactical squad.

Curiosity won, and I sloshed my way through the timber to the other group. There were seven hunters, arrayed in a line a few yards apart, leaning against their respective oaks. I watched them work the next batch of birds.

After one man spotted the flock of mallards off in the distance, five of the seven men began to call. All were good, and the total effect was overpowering. They got the attention of the ducks and swung them our way. When the flock was about 200 yards out, four of the five stopped calling and all seven stopped kicking the water. One man continued to call until the birds were almost overhead, and then he quit.

Peering from beneath my cap brim, I could see the mass of mallards floating lazily past, just above the treetops, necks craning to watch the rippling water down below. When the flock was 100 yards or so past us, the water kicking resumed and the five callers went back into action, and their "comeback" calls were not to be denied. The mallards immediately banked to make another circle.

Four times that flock swept past, with five callers turning them back our way and the one man working them in close.

Then all of the ducks filtered down through the timber to the water, and the shooting began.

The more callers the merrier also applies to goose hunting, again until the flock gets in close. After that one man, or two at the most, can handle the final invitations with more finesse.

Chapter 10

Decoys

A SPREAD OF good decoys, properly set, is perhaps the single most important ingredient for duck and goose hunting success in a majority of the situations encountered in this country. Waterfowl are gregarious by nature, and despite centuries of being lured to their downfall by the imitation birds, ducks and geese continue to respond to this ancient lure.

It *is* ancient. On this continent Indians were fashioning and using artificial duck decoys a thousand years ago, luring them into range of their primitive weapons. Excellent decoys of that period, made of reeds and feathers, have been discovered and preserved.

But it was in the middle of the nineteenth century that the art of making and using artificial decoys was nurtured and developed to a high degree. Market hunters, plying their trade along the Eastern Seaboard, were largely responsible.

The use of live decoys, both ducks and geese, highlighted a colorful era of waterfowling in this country. These Judas birds often seemed to enjoy their work, enthusiastically calling to passing flocks of wild birds. Some would even fly out to mingle with the wild ones, and then lead them back down to the waiting guns.

"It wasn't hard to tell the decoys from the wild ducks," an old market hunter told me. "The tame ducks had a slower wingbeat and a broader breast, so we could keep from shooting them when they flew back in."

Not only could those old-time market hunters shoot, but their eyesight must have been remarkable.

A strong bond developed between many waterfowlers and their live decoys, and when use of the latter was outlawed in 1935 many hunters just quit. Training and using and foolin' with the live birds, according to them, was the most fun of all.

Even when they were legal, live decoys were little used by market gunners shooting the big water of the East Coast. They needed a big spread of decoys to attract flocks from a distance, and handling that many live birds would have been impossible.

Up and down the Mississippi River basin, including the marshes of the Gulf Coast, market hunters frequently used a few live decoys along with a modest spread of artificials. The live birds gave movement and action to the whole rig.

Mud lumps, newspapers, diapers and bottles

Strange items are used as artificial waterfowl decoys from place to place around the continent, and most of them aid success. One of the simplest of all are the mud lumps used

Waterfowl decoys can be very simple—mud lumps turned over by the Cree Indians at James Bay, white rags scattered over a Texas rice field, or newspapers such as this hunter is placing. All are effective some of the time, and none are effective all the time.

by Indians around James Bay, Canada, to lure blue and snow geese.

At the other end of the blue-snow flyway, the marshes of Louisiana, many hunters use newspaper. They twist one corner of a sheet into a "head and neck," and weight down the sheet with a lump of mud. A few dozen of these are amazingly realistic-looking, and the price is right. Another plus is that the newspapers offer little transportation problem.

But they aren't foolproof. Some years ago we were working a newspaper spread and meeting with no success. Time after time a flock would work our way, responding to decoys and calling, only to veer away before coming into gun range. After

an hour or two of this our Cajun guide finally proposed a
reason for our failure: "M'fran, these goose she has already
read yo papers."

In southeast Texas, goose-hunting outfitter Marvin Tyler
owned a restaurant in the small town of Altair. Some years
ago he had a thought, and gathered up all the dirty table
cloths and napkins in his restaurant. Out in the ricefield he
draped these over the rice stubble, lay down among them and
covered himself with a couple of table cloths. He called, and
the geese came right on in—Canadas, blues and snows and
specklebellies. So did pintails and other ducks.

And white-spread hunting became a way of life for gunners around Altair and Eagle Lake. Now the hunters buy
white rags, and use white coveralls and parkas for themselves.

White paper plates and white plastic bleach bottles have
also been used as decoys in place of the rags. Like the newspapers and rags, the plates have the advantage of low cost and
portability. The bottles will work, but it is difficult to carry
any number of them, and they shine in the sun. However,
bleach bottles work fine as floating decoys for ducks, particularly if they're painted. Black—solid black—seems to be about
as good as any color, and it kills the glare from the plastic.
Again, the price is right.

Another shortcut to the real thing is the use of silhouette
decoys, which are simply profiles of ducks or geese in various
attitudes. They don't float, of course, at least not without help,
so are useful largely in the marsh, fields or shallow water
where they can be "stuck up" in the ground. They have the
advantage of portability, since large numbers can be stacked
in a small space, and they can be effective. They are best when
used to complement full-bodied decoys, since when viewed
from above the profiles have no width.

Some ducks and some geese will decoy to almost anything,
but there is no escaping the fact that gunners with the most
realistic decoys have an edge. This is particularly true in areas
which get heavy gun pressure, and becomes progressively

more apparent from the beginning to the end of the hunting season.

Market hunters quickly learned this truism of gunning life, and tried to find the most natural decoys possible. This led to the development of a small coterie of decoy makers who added immeasurably to the distinctive art form in America. The design, carving and painting of the better men were nothing short of works of art, despite their utilitarian origin, and their old decoys are now much in demand by collectors.

Over the years hunters have applied considerable imagination and ingenuity to the subject of decoys, and in the process have devised an interesting array of models, gadgets and techniques. Some have even been practical.

Only one step removed from live decoys was the spread

At the other extreme are mounted birds. These two sandhill crane mounts were used by biologists trying to trap cranes for banding, and they worked when full-bodied artificials didn't.

This flock of sandhill cranes decoys readily to the two mounted birds. The biologists' lack of success using either silhouette or full-bodied artificial decoys seems to indicate exceptional eyesight on the part of the cranes.

of mounted Canada geese which one wealthy sportsman used for a time. They were extremely effective, needless to say, but beyond the financial limitations of most gunners unless they also happened to be taxidermists. An obvious disadvantage to "stuffed" decoys is the care with which they must be handled.

Decoys were or are available which flap their wings, which will "swim" around, and which will dive on command (a pull of the string). They're produced in every attitude imaginable—feeding, tipping, resting, loafing, alert. And they're constructed of wood, cork, plastic, paper, aluminum, steel and rubber.

The type of decoy which is best for any one hunter depends

largely upon where and how he hunts. If he must set and retrieve his decoys at the beginning and end of each hunt, reason dictates a sensible limit to the number of blocks he should use. How he must transport the decoys to the shooting site will obviously play a major role in the type and number of decoys which are practical.

Collapsible decoys made of rubber are the ultimate in lightness and portability, for a hunter can carry a dozen or so in his coat with little effort. In some circumstances this factor can far outweigh the superior appearance of heavier, bulkier decoys.

How many decoys?

There are few situations in which it's possible to use too many decoys. As a general rule, the bigger your spread the greater the attraction for ducks. However, in most locations a point of diminishing return is usually evident.

If you hunt big water, use more decoys. From one hundred to three hundred decoys is probably average for permanent blinds on large lakes and bays, when the decoys don't have to be set and retrieved each day. In many areas they can be left out throughout the season, which frees the gunner to use as many as his pocketbook and inclination dictate.

If the decoys must be set out and picked up each day, *I* would never use that many, no matter how big the water. It becomes a chore which almost overwhelms the pleasure of the moment. Let your own particular conscience, stamina and dedication be your guide.

On small lakes and marsh ponds one or two dozen decoys is usually adequate. If you drop below that range, however, you do meet a point of diminishing return on the low end. A half-dozen decoys, even in a small pond, aren't as effective as two dozen. But, on the other hand, even two or three decoys are far better than none at all.

On big, open waters large numbers of decoys are often very desirable, with two to four hundred blocks not out of the ordinary. On small ponds and lakes and potholes, or in flooded timber such as this, a half dozen decoys will get the job done.

If I must walk any substantial distance to my shooting area, carrying decoys, I usually take half a dozen of the rubber collapsible kind. When wearing a hunting coat they'll fit right into the game-bag portion. A small backpack is useful for carrying these decoys, too, along with your lunch, camera and extra shells.

The largest number of decoys I've ever gunned over was in an Arkansas ricefield. When the bag limit was dropped down to two mallards per day, Lewis Rush consolidated all of his shooting locations into just one, and put *all* of his decoys around that one setup. We walked out to the pit in darkness, and when dawn came I thought the world had turned to duck

Full-bodied goose decoys may be a bit more effective, but the shell affairs which will nest are extremely convenient. The heads on these are removable, and may be swiveled for a variety of positions.

decoys. Eight hundred blocks makes quite a spread!

"Thought I might just as well let them spend the season out here as back in the shed," Lewis laughed.

I might add that there were few passing flocks which didn't at least make a pass in our direction to see why such a crowd had gathered.

The one big danger in using too many decoys is that you place the edge of the spread out of gun range of your blind. That can tempt flocks to work in, and even light, yet your shooting may be poor. Proper decoy placement will usually eliminate that danger.

Most of the above applies to goose shooting as well as to duck shooting, but where you're using a white spread the more rags you can use the better your shooting will be. Here again the placement of the rags, relative to your shooting positions, is the important thing.

How to place the decoys

Pardon my sacrilege, but I think that the intricate pattern sets advocated by some hunters and many writers are more important to them than to the ducks. With rare exceptions, the wild ducks themselves hew to no rule of thumb in positioning themselves on the water. Neither do geese, on land or water.

In placing a spread of decoys before a blind there is one consideration which I consider of utmost importance: "Invite" decoying flocks to land in a certain spot, a location of your choosing, one which will afford you the best shooting opportunities.

Invite them by leaving an opening in your spread. If you do no more than to split your decoys into two groupings you have increased the effectiveness of your rig substantially. That open water between the groups of decoys, of course, should be in the ideal spot for your shooting.

Decoy placement should be made with a view to making it easy for incoming birds to light. Here an inviting opening has been left in the decoys, at an ideal location for the gunners. Decoy arrangements should be natural for the species involved, but elaborate patterns aren't necessary.

Puddle ducks, especially, don't have any difficulty finding a place to land even in the middle of a multitude of their own kind. They will hover, slip and slide down into the tiniest opening on a crowded pond, if that's necessary. But they also are plagued or blessed with the human characteristic of taking the line of least resistance, which means that they will utilize that open space among the decoys much of the time.

In the case of diving ducks, which land with a sweeping rush which frequently seems completely out of control, a clear landing strip is even more essential. Otherwise, the flock often elects to hit the water outside the decoys, out of range or at marginal range.

If you have a goodly number of decoys, enough to surround or to partially surround your blind, leave a number of such open invitations at key points. Make it easy for incoming birds to land where you prefer them to land.

Leave a couple or three decoys in quite close to your blind, in line with your landing area. This helps to convince incoming birds that there's no danger associated with the abnormal hunk of vegetation. (Or perhaps it just convinces me that I'm convincing the ducks.)

Wind direction is the most important factor in your placement of decoys, simply because most ducks and geese will decoy *into* the wind. If your blind location and type is such that you can shoot in all directions, and can surround the blind with decoys, you are in business no matter what the wind direction happens to be.

If you have a fixed blind location in which you can only shoot toward the north, for instance, then a north wind will cause you problems. Birds will approach the decoys from your rear, and even if they aren't spooked by the back side of the blind, they will present a difficult shooting situation.

Where possible, place your duck decoys downwind from the blind, programming your placement so that the shooting opening is directly downwind and the decoys slightly to either side. If the wind switches during the day, don't hesitate to move some of your rig to compensate.

For reasons known only to the ducks, on some days the birds just won't decoy properly. They come in on one side or the other, pitch in before they reach your setup, or do something else equally frustrating. If you detect this as a pattern on a particular day, shift some of your decoys around to try to cope with it. Repositioning half a dozen blocks can sometimes make a difference, but don't hesitate to make a drastic change if it seems called for.

I don't claim to know what makes ducks and geese tick, especially on some days, and those who do are fooling themselves. How birds act at times has no explanation, not to mortal waterfowl hunters, but odds are good that our feathered friends could tell why if only we could understand.

One move which has worked for me on occasion, when decoying birds were stopping too far out, is to move most of the decoys to the upwind side of the blind. The thought is to make the ducks or geese fly within good gun range on their way to the decoys. For this to be effective, however, your blind must be quite good; otherwise it'll just spook the birds. If it's a pit affair, or at least a very low-level rig, then your chances for success are good.

Positioning of the hunters in white-spread hunting is done that way. The array of white rags is scattered in a general oval shape, with the long axis parallel to the wind direction. Then the hunters lie along the downwind edge of the spread, so that decoying geese will pass directly over them enroute to the main mass of rags. It works because the hunters, lying flat on the ground, are no more conspicuous than the decoys.

In contrast to the sandhill cranes, blue and snow geese will respond even to simple newspaper decoys—at times. This young blue goose was taken in by the "snows" in the foreground.

No blind protrudes up above ground level to deter suspicious birds.

One decoy pattern which has been widely advocated is a long string of blocks running from your main grouping out into the lake, with the philosophy that it will "lead" passing ducks on into your spread. Maybe. Perhaps I just haven't learned the secret, but that just doesn't work for me. As often as birds circle on in to my gun, whether because of or in spite of the "lead" string of decoys, they decide to light somewhere along the string far out of range.

A rather common error is to place decoys too far from the blind. If even the outer fringe of your spread is at the outer limit of good shotgun range, you are handicapped since many birds will tend to land out there.

As a general rule of thumb, make 30 yards from your blind the maximum distance to place your decoys, with the bulk of them even nearer. Then ducks or geese landing just outside the spread will still be within range, while those selecting the open space between your groupings will be perfect.

Many writers and hunters advocate placing some decoys at 40 yards from the blind as an aid in estimating distance. If it helps you, use it, but place only one decoy at 40 yards in a couple of directions, with the main bunch closer in. Some natural object—a tree or bush or clump of marsh grass—is better, but not always available.

It's seldom that I'm able to tear my eyes from decoying birds, even obliquely, to compare their rapidly changing position with that of some object on the water. The exception is in timber shooting, when ducks must physically pass a certain tree on their way to me, in which case their point of no return is obvious.

Browsing about decoys

The use of a "dunker" decoy in your spread can be extremely

effective, and the value increases as the wind velocity decreases. It can be the difference between success and failure when the water is dead calm.

This is nothing more than a method by which the hunter can make a decoy (or more than one decoy) dive beneath the surface, tip up, or move around. It gives a lifelike appearance to the entire spread by creating the kind of waves that are made by feeding or swimming ducks.

The simplest rig of this sort is a wire or string running from the blind to a heavy anchor under the decoy, through a ring or pulley on the anchor, and up to the decoy on the surface. A pull on the string makes the decoy tip up or dive completely beneath the surface.

Another version involves placing one or more decoys on a string to a heavy anchor away from the blind, with another string running from the rear of the decoy to the blind. Lengths of elastic tubing are inserted in one or both strings. A smooth pull on the string stretches the elastic and pulls the decoy toward the blind; when it's released, the decoy "swims" away.

Hunters who shoot in the timber make the ripples of feeding and swimming ducks by kicking the water with hip-booted feet. It's very effective even if the gunner isn't using decoys. With decoys, which get little benefit of wind even if it's blowing, it's even more so.

Watch your decoy and blind area for anything out of normal. A waterlogged decoy tipped slightly sideways may reflect light in a manner frightening to ducks, especially if they approach from one direction. Dead ducks floating belly *down* don't seem to spook incoming birds, and may even help, but belly *up* can mean trouble.

Empty shotshell hulls caught in the blind may flash a warning to ducks or geese, as can tops to thermos bottles and shotgun barrels when the sun is shining.

As you down ducks or geese you may, especially if you're short of decoys, use the dead birds by propping them up in a lifelike position. In shallow water or on land, a forked stick

Many timber shooters start with no decoys, but use the first birds bagged as substitutes. Propped up in this fashion they are natural and effective.

beneath the head of the duck, stuck into the ground, works nicely. When using newspapers, white rags or paper plates for geese, a few real birds propped up here and there really dresses up the spread.

If two of your decoys drift together, move one of them. Not only will the banging together be annoying, especially if they're plastic, but they just won't look right to incoming birds.

It would seem logical that best results would be obtained by using decoys to match the species of birds you're after, but this doesn't always hold true. Most puddle ducks and many diving ducks will decoy readily to mallard and/or pintail decoys.

From a practical standpoint, a hunter can't have a decoy spread for each species, and mixing them helter-skelter isn't the answer. Most of my gunning is for puddle ducks, and I concentrate on mallard and pintail decoys. If shooting the

Geese can be handled in the same way, although the results aren't quite as realistic as with ducks on water.

timber for mallards, I use mallard decoys entirely. In areas where pintails are the dominant species, reason dictates that most or all of the spread should be of pintail decoys.

Many successful gunners swear by the use of a few coot decoys on the fringe of their puddle-duck spread, and I'm inclined to think that this may help. It can't hurt. Others use a few goose decoys, either silhouettes or full-bodies, off to one side or behind the blind.

If you're hunting diving ducks, use diving-duck decoys. Although scaup, ring-necks, cans and redheads will come to puddle-duck blocks, a big spread of their own kind is more effective.

All species of geese will decoy to a white spread, which should tell us something. Canadas, white-fronts, blues and snows will move to the white rags with almost equal abandon —sometimes.

If you have a choice, use the decoys to match the species of geese you're hunting, but keep in mind that you aren't greatly handicapped if that's not possible.

All ducks and geese may not fraternize, but most are nosy enough to detour within gun range of a good decoy spread, no matter what kind they are.

Methods of anchoring and rigging decoys are endless, knowing only the limitless bounds of waterfowlers' ingenuity. There are so many commercial anchors and private versions available that it seems pointless to review them.

Multiple decoy rigs have no appeal for me, since they usually cause me more grief than they afford utility or speed. Other hunters use them and like them, which is why some people buy Fords and some Chevrolets.

One modern-day advantage which old-time duck hunters missed is the availability of monofilament as an anchor line for decoys in very deep water. Braided nylon is easiest to handle and best for shallow-water sets, but the mono is a blessing for the deep stuff. And, particularly in bulk spools, it is very inexpensive.

Two tips for retrieving decoys. One is to cut a small notch in the blade of your paddle (or oar or pushpole) which will catch the decoy line. The other is a godsend on a windy day. Drop your boat anchor *upwind* from your spread and play out line as needed to reach the decoys. It'll save a lot of upwind paddling—or motor running—to get back into position.

To ensure long life and good service from decoys, take care of them. A bit of maintenance and proper storage between hunting seasons is worth the effort.

Chapter 11

Retrievers

WATERFOWL RETRIEVERS, like waterfowl hunters, come in a full assortment of sizes, shapes, colors and dispositions. One of the most interesting I've ever gunned over was a mousy-looking Chesapeake that looked like something a Lab dragged in. She was small, maybe fifty pounds, with all of the drive and enthusiasm of a drunk headed to the tank for the umpteenth time.

When the flock of mallards swept into sight over the fringe of trees lining the intracoastal canal, Rod and R. J. opened up with their calls in a medley which was solid music. Blending highballs and greetings with an ease that bespoke long practice, they wove a magic spell of notes which would not

The Labrador is by far the most popular retriever in the nation. It has an excellent disposition, can handle all waterfowl including the big Canada goose, and works extremely well on dry-land retrieving.

be denied. After one quick circle the dozen birds peeled off and came on in.

We chopped five of them down, the last to fall a slanting bird with just a wingtip broken. Through all the action the little Chesapeake sat calmly on the boat seat, smothered by the blind and unable to see a thing. She wasn't bored with it all, I don't suppose, but neither was she uptight.

"Get on outta here and get a bird." Rod shoved the dog toward a small hole in the rosseau cane of the blind.

Some retrievers hit the water with a smashing splash. This one figuratively tested the water with a paw, then shivered her way overboard with scarcely a ripple. In no time she was back with a greenhead, which Rod accepted with, "Go get another one."

Shooting over very thick marsh vegetation, we killed three limits of ducks and lost none. The Chesapeake retrieved them

Dogs are individuals. Most Chesapeakes are aggressive and eager, hitting the water with a splash. This one figuratively tested it with a paw before easing overboard, but she also retrieved three limits of ducks in difficult terrain without losing a bird.

all. When I asked Rod about her attitude, he replied, "Yeah, she likes to hunt. She'll be in the truck each morning before I get my gun. But she just doesn't make a big deal about bringing back ducks. I really don't think she likes t'get wet."

Few will deny that the use of a dog increases the pleasure of most hunting expeditions. That's true whether the quarry is quail, grouse, pheasant, rabbits, fox, raccoon or woodcock. Even with deer, in some sections of the nation, there are hunters who would rather stay home than do without the music of their hounds.

A dog isn't essential to the success of some of these, even if it does add the frosting to the gunner's pleasure. Neither is a retriever essential to the success of most waterfowling, but a day afield with a good one lifts a hunt from the realm of good to that of great.

Even more important, use of retrievers for waterfowling saves countless birds each year which would otherwise be lost. More than three million ducks killed by hunters go unretrieved each fall, a really frightful loss of a precious resource.

The nature of the sport makes it easy to lose dead ducks, because of the thick vegetation found around many shooting areas. Birds which drop only crippled, of course, are doubly difficult to retrieve—without a dog.

Because of their size and because of the type of terrain on which they're normally hunted, the percentage loss of downed geese is lower than for ducks. Even so, more than two hundred thousand geese are killed but lost each year.

I've mentioned how very much a "good" retriever adds to a hunt, and I want to emphasize that adjective. The dog need not be of trial caliber, nor have all the spit and polish of the drawing room, but to be enjoyable a retriever *must* be manageable.

Some of my most unpleasant experiences have been days of gunning with men whose dogs were out of control. Such animals will completely negate the pleasures of the moment, and often render the bagging of ducks or geese out of the question. It isn't their fault.

"You blankety-blank, hard-headed s.o.b." is the first reaction most of us have to a dog that won't mind. I've not only thought it; I've said just that, a time or two. But the thought should have been directed to the dog's owner, which in a couple or three of those situations was me.

Retrievers have more or less innate ability and instinct to retrieve, are more or less aggressive, and have varying levels of a desire to please. But beyond that, beyond those basics, the manner in which they perform in the field depends entirely upon the training they have had.

Some hunters aren't dog people

Not all of us can play the piano or sing, which is no discredit. Some hunters, in the same vein, are not geared to own or handle retrievers. They simply don't have the patience, self-control, and/or—let's face it—intelligence to cope with a hunting dog.

One session I experienced some years back in a duck blind will live in infamy. For three hours I squirmed and suffered while Mr. X screamed at a bewildered, nine-month-old Lab: *"Get back in this blind! . . . Leave that damn decoy alone! . . . Where th' hell you going? . . . No! No!! That way! That way! . . . You stupid son of a bitch!"*

There are college graduates who couldn't have understood his directions, or even what he was saying. The poor dog was destroyed, ignorant as to what he should do and completely unable to understand why his master was so unhappy.

Retrievers have a natural instinct to retrieve or, more accurately, to run or swim out and pick something up and come back with it. It's an inborn reaction in the dog, something he likes to do. But he may drop the object before he gets back, he may take it in the other direction, or he may come back but not give it to you.

"Naw, ole Rover never had any training. He's just a natural retriever."

Some dogs, with some masters, do become acceptable gun dogs with little or no formal training. In those instances the temperament of the owner is such that the dog is able to determine, to a degree, what the man wants. That, combined with the retriever's natural retrieving instinct and his desire to please, results in a fair to good gun dog.

The value of "forced" training to retrieve, as opposed to merely depending upon the inherited instinct of the dog, is great. With the latter, there inevitably comes a day when your retriever decides he doesn't want to go after a bird. Or, having found the duck, he decides he doesn't want to bring it back to the blind. At that point the hunter has no way to make that "natural retriever" do his bidding. With a dog which was force-trained, the hunter can *make* him retrieve.

Don't punish without prior training

A cardinal, inflexible rule of training or handling a dog of any kind, including retrievers, is: *Never punish a dog for failing to do something he hasn't been trained to do.* That seems elementary, something that no reasonable man would do, but the fact is that a great many hunters do make that mistake.

The second canon of dog training, especially retriever training, is: *You cannot teach a dog anything unless it is under control.* That means simply that your retriever, first of all, must be obedient. Only after he has learned obedience can you teach him to retrieve ducks and geese.

The ultimate pleasure

Assuming that you are temperamentally competent to handle a retriever, which most people are once they understand the rules, and that you have a dog which has been properly trained, then the use of a retriever in duck and goose hunting is one of the ultimate pleasures in waterfowling. It quickly becomes such a vital part of the affair that its absence makes the gunning a bit on the bland side, like a good roast without seasoning. It's still good, and most enjoyable, but the spice is gone.

The enthusiasm and drive with which a jam-up retriever

Although not quite as good for land work, the Chesapeake Bay retriever has no peer in the water. Extremely rugged and usually aggressive, it handles severe cold situations with ease. Here the hunter gives his Chesapeake the line to a downed bird.

works is marvelous to behold. A Lab hitting the water is a thrilling sight, and the way many retrievers perform makes it obvious that they "think." How else can you explain a dog which will ignore dead ducks in his path to go for a cripple which falls out of sight in the grass?

Nickie, a golden retriever owned by Marvin Tyler, of Altair, Texas, is phenomenal. If a goose is missed, he ignores it completely. If it's hit but keeps flying, this dog will watch the bird for hundreds of yards to make sure it isn't (or is) going down, sometimes trotting along in that direction for forty or fifty yards. He has bird and hunting sense that is uncanny, and is completely under Marvin's control at all times.

That he retrieves several thousand ducks and geese each

Second in popularity to the Lab is the golden retriever. This one is Nickie, owned by Marvin Tyler of Altair, Texas, and for my money he is one of the better gun dogs in the nation. Here Nickie watches a disappearing flock of geese for signs of a cripple.

season doesn't hurt, but not even massive opportunity such as that results in exceptional performance from all dogs.

Pet or hunting dog?

There is a widespread belief that no dog which is a pet, especially a house pet, can be a good hunting dog. This is certainly not the case with retrievers.

In the early 1970's the winner of the National Retriever Trial, the world series of retrieverdom, was a black Labrador named Creole Sister. She is the house pet and bosom companion of the Don Weisses, of Shreveport, Louisiana. Not only that, but she was also handled in the trial by Don, who is an attorney, not a professional trainer. No other female retriever, in field-trial history, has ever won more trial points.

A retriever, obviously, can be both a pet and a fine hunting dog.

But, you say, all field-trial champions aren't necessarily good hunting dogs. In the case of some breeds, notably the pointing dogs, this is true. With retrievers, however, a good trial dog is always a good hunting dog.

The reason for this is found in the manner in which retrievers are expected to work on ducks and geese. They are to sit or lie in or near the blind, boat or pit, preferably at a location where they can mark down birds, and remain there until given the signal to retrieve. Then they are expected to go quickly to the area of the fall, find the bird, and bring it directly back to the blind.

That is exactly what field-trial champs must do. The trial dog, however, is set apart from most gun dogs in that it must be able to mark and remember multiple falls, take precise direction from hand and whistle signals, and perform with verve and dash sufficient to win over the judges.

All of these fringe qualities, of course, make that retriever even more valuable and exciting as a hunting dog.

PHOTO COURTESY FLORIDA DEVELOPMENT COMMISSION

The springer spaniel isn't known particularly as a waterfowl retriever, but will do a fine job under many conditions. Springers are at their best on dry-land or shallow-water situations like this pass-shooting location in Minnesota.

The *average* retriever over which I've gunned around the nation is not required to hold fast after the bird is shot. He is expected and required to remain steady until the shooting begins, but then he is free to move out to retrieve.

That average dog will take general hand direction, especially if you throw an empty shotshell in the direction in which the duck fell, and will come back in when his master demands. He will, in short, sit, fetch and come, and those three qualities make him a worthwhile companion in the field.

A retriever is much more valuable, of course, if he has more of the trial dog's capabilities. Being steady to shot has several advantages, the first being that the dog can then mark down *all* of the birds that fall, not just the first one. If a duck or goose falls crippled, the steady dog can be sent for that bird first to minimize its chances of escaping.

Another plus of a retriever which goes only on command is that there may be more birds on the way to your decoys. If the dog breaks to shot, there's a fair to good chance that he will spook those additional birds.

The gun dog which can take direction, as a trial dog must, is worth more money. The hunter, ideally, can send the retriever off on the proper line, which the dog will follow until he finds the bird or is stopped by the master; he can stop the dog at any point; and from any point he can direct the dog left, right, back or in. Only the degree and style with which a retriever can do these things separate the good gun dogs from the field-trial champions.

Can I train my own retriever?

Any average hunter can train his retriever to be an acceptable, enjoyable gun dog—*if* he has the time and patience, and *if* he will make the effort. Only you can determine whether or not you fit that mold.

Many excellent books are available on how to train hunt-

Retriever training isn't difficult, but it requires time and the right temperament. The satisfaction of a retrieve such as this is worth the effort it required.

ing dogs, including retrievers, and several are included in the book list at the end of this book. Whether you train your own dog or not, get one or more of these books and familiarize yourself with the training techniques.

There are professional trainers throughout the country who will train your retriever for you. As with any other trade or profession, they come in all degrees of competence and incompetence. Before handing your dog over to one, request references and check with people who have had the man (or woman) train their dogs.

One of the top trainers in the nation is Bert Carlson, of Issaquah, Washington, a suburb of Seattle. He isn't exactly typical, since he has a master's degree in chemistry from the University of Washington, plus an additional three years in medical school. At that point his love of dogs won out over a career in either chemistry or medicine, and he now has the biggest kennel in that part of the country.

Bert will train any breed, but specializes in retrievers and has become recognized as one of the best. He has sold retrievers for as much as $10,000, and has placed high in the national trials. His comments about training retrievers, in other words, deserve attention.

"Training a retriever," said Bert, "is like climbing the rungs of a ladder. You must take them one at a time. You can't start at the top, which so many hunters try to do."

One of Bert's pet peeves is the writer or trainer who insists on one set routine: "Most dog writers and dog books are too dogmatic. There isn't any one right way to handle and train a dog. Retrievers are just too different, and the good trainer must be able to recognize these differences."

The schedule which Bert prefers to follow in training a hunting retriever is simple. He wants the dog for one month when the dog is about six to eight months of age for obedience training, and then for one more month at about one year of age for field finishing. At that point the dog should be an acceptably good hunting dog which is steady, will take a straight line and retrieve to hand, has a soft mouth, and will come on signal.

When pups are six to eight weeks old, according to Bert, you can get a good idea of just how eager they'll be. At that point he plays with a litter with a live pigeon to see if the dogs are "birdy," as he calls it, a term indicating eagerness when they're confronted with a bird. At that same age he starts getting them used to the sound of a gun. Working them one by one, he throws a pigeon out on the grass, and after the pup has picked up the bird Bert fires a blank pistol. Gradually he fires the pistol earlier, until finally he is firing it and then throwing the bird.

When he is sure a pup is birdy and not gunshy, he sells it, and has the owner take it home. "I want the dog to get used to his people, get to love the man he'll be hunting for. The owner can do a little obedience training all along, nothing serious, then bring the dog back to me at about six or eight months."

Between the month of obedience training with Bert and the month of field finishing, the owner must regularly work with the dog on the obedience lessons he has already learned. Bert requires that the owner, if at all possible, spend some time with him and the dog, learning the commands and techniques which the retriever has grown used to.

Commands—short and consistent

Wrong: "You better get on back in here!"
Right: "COME!"

Wrong: "Don't you dare move!"
Right: "STAY!"

Wrong: "Keep in here close. Stay with me."
Right: "HEEL!"

Wrong: "Go get that bird."
Right: "BACK!"

Wrong: "You stop right there."
Right: "SIT!"

The point is that you make the vocabulary with which you communicate with your retriever short, clear and always the same. It is the word itself which should get the right response, perhaps with a certain voice inflection, although that mitigates against the use of the dog by others. Don't depend upon the harshness of your voice to command obedience. Don't, in other words, scream.

The commands are largely self-explanatory. "Heel" means that the dog should stay at your side (usually the left side) no matter where you move. "Back" is the command most often used to send the dog out on a retrieve, and is usually accompanied by a thrust of the handler's hand from a point near the dog's head out toward the bird. "Sit" means for the dog to stop where he is and to sit. Some hunters prefer "Whoa." Just be consistent.

"Down" is an extension of "Sit," and means just what it says. Some teach it; some don't. It's useful to make the dog lie down in a boat (tippy pirogue), blind, auto or home.

Whistle signals

Although I don't enjoy the sound of a whistle on my duck lake or goose field, since it is an artificial sound completely foreign to the outdoors, there is no denying the value of a whistle in working a retriever. All trial dogs are handled by whistle, which alone is firm evidence of their effectiveness.

Why? Because a whistle can be heard by your dog farther than your voice can, especially if there is a wind blowing. And because you can blow a whistle with much less effort than you can shout a command—which is as good a time as any to caution against too many commands. Use those you need, but no more, and that applies both to the whistle and to your voice.

Whistle signals are used largely for two commands: a sharp *"toot!"* means stop, the equivalent of the voice command "Sit"; and a drawn out *"rooty-toot-toot"* means for the dog to come to you, the equivalent of "Come."

The sharp *"toot!"* really means more than just stop. It should tell the dog to stop, sit and look at you for direction. But there is one difficulty with using just that to stop a running, plunging, sloshing dog which has his mind made up. That short noise is often too brief for the dog to hear, thus he can't heed it.

The solution is to give a drawn-out whistle, which gets the dog's attention, and end it with that sharp toot. Something like, *"toooooooooootoot!!"* The first part warns the dog that a command is coming, and the last part gives it.

Hand signals

The most useful hand signal for most hunters is the one which shows the dog the direction to the bird, which trainers call the "line." Have your retriever at sit position on your left side, facing the bird, and with your left hand near his head slowly point with it directly along the line. Then do it vigorously, simultaneously giving the command "Back!" and the dog will be off in the right direction.

Progressing to hand signals beyond this point is for the more finished dog, but these more advanced signals are very valuable, and are surprisingly easy to teach. They just require more time and patience.

The additional hand signals are for the purpose of directing your retriever from a point out away from your blind: (1) to the right; (2) to the left; or (3) farther away from you. For right and left you simply step and point in the appropriate direction, giving the command "Over!" To send him farther away, step toward the dog and thrust one hand directly overhead, giving the command "Back!"

The immense value of being able to give such commands is obvious, since with them you can direct your dog to the exact area of a bird. To give them, of course, you must first be able to make your dog stop and look at you; otherwise he cannot see your signals.

Don't lie to your retriever, ever! Never send him to retrieve a bird or a dummy which isn't there. You must build into him a confidence that you can and will help direct him to the bird, but only if he needs help.

As Bert Carlson emphasizes over and over, "You don't train a dog by correction, by punishment." Correction is justified and effective only with a recalcitrant dog which doesn't do something he has already been trained to do. You must be sure the dog knows what you want him to do, and how to do it, before meting out any punishment for failure.

Important: After you correct your retriever, immediately let him know you're still his friend. Don't stay "mad" at the dog for making a mistake.

The cost of letting a professional train your dog will probably be somewhere around $100 a month for the two months Carlson recommends, which includes board, training aids (pigeons, ducks, pheasants) and lessons. For advanced training beyond that point the cost is somewhat higher, which is understandable since the trainer must devote more time to finishing the product.

To repeat, there is little mystery and enormous satisfaction in training your own retriever to be a good hunting dog. You need time and patience, and a working knowledge of how to train a retriever, which you can learn from any of the good training books. And, you must have a dog!

Which retriever should I get?

The listing of species and breeds and critters which have been used to fetch things for their masters over the ages is long. It includes such unlikely candidates as hounds and terriers and mongrels, and even pigs. A hunting buddy of mine in Arizona, Curt Earl, had a something with overtones of chow, collie and shepherd which would do anything he asked, which included retrieving quail, doves or rabbits. Bob Brister, a Houston friend who is Shooting Editor of *Field & Stream,* has

A Lab makes easy work of a snow goose. Crippling loss of waterfowl is very high, and would be reduced substantially if all hunters used good retrievers.

a Cairn terrier which is a fine retriever on game to match his size.

But if you're going to get a dog especially for retrieving waterfowl, don't get a pig. Or a Cairn, chow, collie or shepherd. Get a recognized retriever breed.

The ranking retrievers, in the order of their popularity, are the Labrador, the golden and the Chesapeake Bay retrievers. All of them make excellent gun dogs.

All three of these breeds normally range from 60 to 75 pounds in weight, and stand 20 to 26 inches at the shoulder. The golden will average the smallest of the three, the Chesapeake the largest, and the Lab in between. Females are generally smaller than males.

The Lab is not only the most popular retriever in America, but also one of the most popular dogs, regardless of breed. His efficiency at retrieving (Labs dominate retriever trials), fine disposition, versatility at hunting upland birds as well as waterfowl, and his short, clean coat are responsible. The latter attribute is especially attractive to wives, particularly if the Lab is a house pet.

The golden has most of the fine qualities of the Labrador, plus a longer, silky coat which makes this the most handsome of the retrievers. Excellent in the upland fields as a flushing-retrieving dog, the popularity of this breed will continue to rise.

The Chesapeake Bay retriever, one of only two breeds of gun dogs developed in this country, has no equal at water retrieving. Tremendously powerful swimmers, they also have a thick, oily coat which protects them even in icy waters. The latter quality doesn't help the Chesapeake as a house dog, and neither does a temperament which is strong-willed, independent and aggressive. "If he gets into my favorite chair first," was the way one Chesapeake Bay owner told it, "I don't try to move him." This breed is not as good as a Lab or a golden on land work, or for upland birds, but its stamina, courage, ruggedness and intelligence make it a marvel at retrieving from water.

Other breeds which work well on waterfowl include the Irish water spaniel, the American water spaniel, the curly-coated retriever, and the flat-coated retriever. All would be considered big dogs except for the American water spaniel, which ranges from 25 to 40 pounds in weight and 15 to 18 inches at the shoulder.

The low level of popularity of the American is an enigma, since this is one of the most versatile of our hunting dogs. As John Falk wrote in *The Practical Hunter's Dog Book,* " ... this

A trained retriever under control, *like this Lab, is a joy. One which is unmanageable is a complete disaster. The first lesson which a prospective dog trainer should take to heart is that it is impossible to teach a retriever anything unless the dog is under control.*

little gun dog shows a penchant for hunting virtually any small game species that swims, runs, hops or flies."

This dog has the disposition desired in a house pet, the moderate size which is a plus in cramped living quarters or tiny pirogues, and the swimming ability and toughness to make the retrieve, and he is an excellent flush dog for upland game. One of my finest memories is gunning woodcock over the American water spaniel which belonged to my treasured New Orleans hunting companion, Elemore Morgan.

That ability to double in brass for other types of hunting is one quality which has made some of the retriever breeds so popular. They can be trained to hunt at heel until the bird is flushed and shot, often over pointing dogs, then used to retrieve. Or they can be used as flushing dogs, spaniel-like, on pheasants, woodcock, grouse and quail. They make excellent dove retrievers.

Try it

If your situation permits, get a retriever. Before making a decision you might want to attend a retriever trial, many of which are held throughout the nation. There you'll see mostly Labs, perhaps some goldens, but you'll be exposed to the kind of performance a fine retriever can deliver.

Then get your dog, be it pup or finished product. When the day and hour arrives that you give him that "Back!" on his first wild duck, and he fetches it from the lake to your hand, a new era in your waterfowling pleasure will have begun.

Chapter 12

Clothes and Other Gear

CLOTHING FOR WATERFOWLING should be capable of keeping the hunter warm, dry, camouflaged and comfortable. A vast array of products is now available which covers the gamut of gunning situations and touches all the above bases, yet I'm constantly amazed at how many ill-equipped duck and goose hunters I encounter.

The reason for this is twofold: First, sporting goods stores in small towns (and often in the larger ones, too) don't stock much of a selection; and secondly, the gunner waits until the last moment before attempting to buy what he needs. The solution is to plan ahead and buy early, affording plenty of time to shop around to locate the right items. Then if you

The three-quarter-length parka, in camouflage or in dead-grass color, is one of the most useful duck-hunting garments. Waterproof and windproof, it has an attached hood, and will keep a hip-booted hunter completely dry. It should be cut full enough so that heavy clothes can be worn beneath it if necessary.

can't find what you want locally, you'll have time to order from a mail-order house.

These mail-order catalog houses collectively offer the sportsman an enormous range of choice. Some of the best known, most reputable of these are listed at the end of this chapter, and will send a catalog upon request.

To start at the bottom, I wear some type of "long-handles" when I duck or goose hunt if the weather is at all cool. The conditions surrounding waterfowling usually make it seem colder than the temperature would indicate. You're on or around water, and dampness increases the chill effect; you are stashed in one place, a blind or pit, which eliminates moving around to generate warmth; and your physical position frequently is a cramped one, which further reduces circulation and contributes to that cold, clammy feeling.

My favorite such underwear is the two-piece "Duofold" type, which has a layer of cotton next to the skin and a layer of wool on the outside. Get them bigger than normal, since they tend to shrink after repeated washings, and creepy, crawly underwear isn't welcome in a duck blind.

If I don't need quite that much protection, I use the mesh-type, again the two-piece. In *very* severe weather, I go to the goosedown underwear, which gives the ultimate protection but which also gives me a very stuffed feeling.

The top of down underwear, by the way, doubles very nicely as a light jacket. Be careful of rips, however, since its outer fabric isn't designed against them.

For cold-weather protection the usual advice is that several light layers are better than one heavy layer. That's true, largely because the air space between the layers also gives protection. It is also practical, since layers can be removed or added as conditions warrant. However, there is a practical limit to this strategy.

After much trial and considerable error, I've arrived at several combinations which seem to cover most of my duck and goose gunning situations. Perhaps some of them will work for you.

My outer garment for most waterfowling is a three-quarter-length parka which is waterproof, windproof and camouflage-colored, and which has a hood attached. It does not give a great deal of warmth, but protects from rain, sleet, snow and wind, which makes it practical even in moderate weather.

What I wear beneath that parka, between it and the long johns, is determined by the weather and the shooting conditions. For moderate weather: wool whipcord pants and a wool shirt. For cool to cold weather: medium-weight wool pants (27.5-ounce) and a wool shirt, plus a down shirt which is really

The outer clothing for white spread hunting is simple—white coveralls with a white hood. What goes on underneath is up to you. The white-clad hot-shots flanking Marvin Tyler above are Andy Griffith and Sam Snead.

a light jacket. For very cold conditions: heavy wool pants (32 ounce), a wool shirt and a down jacket. I am being rather specific so that you will know exactly the type, style and weight garments which do the job for me.

All of the wool pants are cut full, are very tough, and have great ability to shed rain and snow. All have at least one hip pocket which has a button, and preferably a flap which buttons.

There are many fine wool shirts on the market. Most of mine are the Pendleton-type, which have the features I like. They are medium-weight and are cut full with a long tail which will stay in your pants, and they have pockets with buttoned flaps. The button may seem like a small thing, but not when it keeps you from losing a duck call, compass, chap stick, notebook or whatever you stash in a breast pocket.

These shirts also have another important feature: the neck is lined with smooth nylon, which prevents chafing during the many, many times a hunter turns his head to look for birds during a day. If the neck isn't lined (it is little trouble to sew one in), try using a turtleneck pullover under the wool shirt. Regardless of the shirt I'm wearing, I frequently wear a polyester, cotton, or soft-wool pullover beneath it for additional warmth, and particularly for the protection it affords around the neck area.

For warm-weather waterfowling I use cotton or poplin pants and shirt, in either camouflage or tan as the situation warrants.

Another garment which is becoming very popular is the

The insulated coverall worn by hunter on the right is a handy item for wildfowlers, though the traditional khaki hunting coat remains a favorite with many duck hunters. Blue jeans and short boots are great if you've got webbed feet, but I'd settle for the waders.

one-piece suit, frequently called a "jump suit" or coverall. They are available in all weights, including those insulated with synthetics and with down, in camouflage and in solid colors. These suits have the advantage of almost instantly changing a man from whatever he is wearing into hunting garb. They are indeed "coveralls."

If you buy one of these suits, make sure that the full-length zipper up and down the front is a two-way zipper, one that opens from the bottom as well as the top. That can be important when a hunter needs to make a pit stop out in the blind.

It is also an advantage in such a suit to have zippers up each leg. That permits you to put it on and take it off without removing your boots.

Footgear

Under most waterfowling conditions rubber is the best material for footgear, since it is the best protection against water.

The hip boot is *the* type of footgear favored by most waterfowlers around the nation, and that's understandable. It gives a surprising degree of warmth, protection against getting the feet wet even when wading two-foot-deep waters, and protection from rain or snow for the part of your body below your "rain" parka.

Wearing hip boots and my three-quarter-length parka, I'm equipped to handle any weather.

If you're gunning waters where there is no need to wade, then short rubber boots are a bit more comfortable than hip boots. But even in hunting situations where we step right from the boat into the blind and do all our retrieving with dog or boat, one of our party will usually wear the longer boots. There are just so many instances in duck or goose hunting when it is an advantage to be able to step off into knee-deep water—to shove a boat free, to retrieve a bird, to right a decoy, to take a picture.

Shooting ducks and geese from land does not usually call for hip boots. "Short" rubber boots, of course, can have 6-inch tops or 18-inch tops, so choose the length best suited to your situation.

At the other extreme are waders, which reach to the gunner's waist or to his chest. They are great for wading flooded timber, and in many marsh situations where the water depth varies quite a bit. Waders are perfect for sitting or kneeling in shallow marsh, which is frequently one of the best ways to hunt when ducks or geese are blind-shy. However, they can be dangerous if a canoe or piroque dunks you, for they're tricky to shed in a hurry.

For warm-weather hunting you may prefer the lightweight stocking-foot wader, available in nylon or inexpensive plastics. With these, you wear a shoe of some kind over the wader. Regular sneakers will do, although specialized wading shoes are available.

Short boots, hip boots and waders are available in many styles. Your first consideration should be the choice between insulated and noninsulated boots, which will obviously be governed by the temperature when and where you hunt. Most duck and goose hunters end up having both kinds.

Another choice is between regular boot lasts and the "ankle-fit" kind. The latter are best if much walking is involved, and especially so on muddy terrain which tends to pull your boot off at each step. Ankle-fits are not as comfortable for long hours in the blind, and they aren't as warm since they must be tight around the ankles, and people with unusually high insteps may find them uncomfortable.

One gimmick you can use to make any boot an "ankle-fit" model is to use a cross-section of an old innertube on each foot. Put it around your ankle, cross it over your instep, and stretch it over your toe to the small of your foot.

Headgear

A cap or hat with a visor is quite important in waterfowling. That brim gives you something to peer from behind, to hide that face from the penetrating eyes of ducks and geese.

Keep in mind that a man's extremities are where his body loses heat most quickly, thus it is necessary to protect them as fully as possible in order to keep warm. Feet, head and hands.

For cold weather your best bet is an insulated cap with ear flaps. I have several, geared to various weather conditions, including one insulated with down. Those ear flaps are great for extreme conditions, but they bug me no end. I like to hear the sounds of the lake and the marsh, and ear flaps prevent that to a degree.

If my ears are getting too cold, my first reaction is to put my hood up, to knock off the wind. Since it's difficult or impossible to use a hood if you're wearing a hat, I wear caps.

There are several kinds of "watch caps" or "stocking caps" on the market which have merit for some situations. The "Balaclava" type can be worn up in the Navy watch-cap fashion, protecting the head; it can be rolled all the way down to protect head, ears and neck, with an opening for the face; or it can be pulled up over the chin to protect the mouth and nose, leaving only the eyes free.

Another is a separate hood and dickey, which can be worn with any coat or jacket. Insulated with goose down, it has a visor, and it gives great protection to head, ears, neck and chest. The dickey part fits under your jacket or coat in front and in back.

The point is that there are many hat and cap styles available for waterfowlers, with the widest choice available from the mail-order houses. Look around until you find just what *you* need.

Handgear

As with headgear, many, many types of gloves and mittens are available to cover various shooting conditions. With outer shells of cotton, wool, plastic or leather, lined or unlined, the wide array provides quite a choice for those who will look.

I am fond of thin leather "shooting gloves," but they don't afford much protection from cold. They give a nonslip grip and are sensitive enough to let you handle shells easily, but most will soak up water like a sponge. If it is wet *and* cold, bad news.

Anything that keeps your hands from making contact with the cold wood and metal of your gun is a lot of protection. Even the very inexpensive cotton gloves available everywhere (about 50 cents a pair) are a big help. I'll often take along two or three pairs of these, switching them when one gets wet.

Wool gloves are quite warm, and remain fairly good protection even when wet, but don't give much gun feel. Some wool gloves have palms and fingers faced with leather to cope with the "feel" problem, but it's a compromise.

Mittens are the warmest kind of handgear, and the warmest combination of all is a leather outer mitten and a wool inner mitten. That's what I use in extremely cold weather, slipping the right one off, quick and easy, for shooting. Some shooting mittens have a slit in the right one for the trigger finger.

For handling decoys in cold weather, get a pair of waterproof gloves. A good bet is the plastic-coated glove which, although worthless for shooting, is very inexpensive.

Most of the time, even in very cold weather, I seem to end up in the blind or pit without any gloves on my hands. Between flights they're stuck in my jacket pockets, often wrapped around hand warmers. If I must keep one hand free to hold a gun, I'll usually keep a glove or mitten on the left one for that purpose, and keep the shooting hand in the pocket.

No duck call sounds as good when blown from a gloved hand. The glove or mitten has a muffling effect. With goose calls this isn't as critical.

Raingear

That three-quarter-length parka mentioned above is my usual raingear, with nothing else needed if I'm wearing hip boots. Without hip boots, I'll take along the pants of a rain suit.

About that rain suit—if the weather is moderate, with little prospect of precipitation, and/or if the hunt involves a lot of walking (which the long parka isn't ideal for), I take along a tough, lightweight, fully waterproof rain suit. The pants and top (which has a built-in hood) of the suit will roll into a very small space, which fits easily into my shell bucket, backpack, duffle bag, or into the game pocket if I'm wearing a hunting coat.

Rain suits are available in all ranges of quality and weight, in camouflage and in various solid shades of green and brown. Pick the one which suits your needs best.

Take rain gear with you on *every* hunt, no matter how clear and bright the sky. Winter weather can and does change in a very short time, so be prepared to cope with those changes. Not only are rainproof garments great for keeping you dry, but their windproof qualities add tremendously to the warming potential of your other clothing.

Other Gear

There are times when a waterfowler puts shells in his pockets, a duck call around his neck, picks up his shotgun and is ready to go hunting. Most of us, however, tote quite a bit more excess baggage along, which brings up the decision as to how to carry it.

For situations where they are practical, the greatest item to fill this bill is called a shell bucket. I don't know where their use originated, but in the marshes of Louisiana they are a fixture.

The typical "bucket" has a solid wooden bottom, a lid made of plywood, and sides constructed of vertical wooden strips. It is round, and has a handle for carrying. For water-fowling they are painted a dull brown, green, olive or camou-flage. I fiberglass mine inside around the bottom, and up the

Shell bucket, made from a firkin, carries the many miscellaneous items which are necessary to a duck hunter: shells, rain gear, thermos, duck calls, lunch, camera, extra gloves, handwarmer, and binoculars. Down jackets worn by these two hunters are excellent cold-weather protection for waterfowlers.

sides a few inches, to make them completely waterproof even after sitting in water in the boat or blind for hours.

Most of these shell buckets are manufactured in the New England states. They are firkins, small wooden casks once used for butter or lard, but now largely for such things as sewing baskets. The man who first began using a firkin for a shell bucket must live in anonymity, but he deserves a medal.

Right now I could pluck my shell bucket from the shelf, grab my gun, and be ready to hunt. In it I carry shells, calls, rainsuit, handwarmer and fluid, pair of gloves, mosquito repellent, snakebite kit, small pair of binoculars, chap stick, a thermos, boot-repair stick, matches, aspirin, Band-Aids, and a small camera. Most of those items remain in the bucket at all times, with camera, binocs and thermos about the only exceptions.

Another plus for the shell bucket is that it can be used as a seat. It is especially useful when shooting from a boat. Placed on the boat seat, it usually puts your head about level with the top of the blind, which is just right.

A few years ago some company produced a plastic shell bucket in the shape of the firkin, which is bigger at the bottom than at the top, but they were of poor quality and apparently have vanished from the scene. A very good-quality "fishing" item which some hunters now use as a shell bucket is the Tackle Seat made by Woodstream.

The Tackle Seat is made of rugged ABS plastic and has a hinged lid-seat. It has an insulated bottom compartment which can be used for food or beverages or ice, with two removable trays above. The insulated compartment, of styrofoam, can be removed if you prefer to use that space for something else.

Another solution is to carry your gear in a duffle bag of sorts. Converse-Hodgeman has an inexpensive one called the Carry-All Duffle Bag, 30x13 inches, which is roomy and waterproof, with a rope drawstring at the top. I use them as a "boat bag" for fishing and also for hunting. There's room in them to stuff in your jacket when the weather warms up. Orvis has a similar, more expensive 11x25-inch bag which is very good.

A third handy idea, especially if you must walk a good distance, is a backpack. It frees the hands for carrying gun, decoys and other things.

A sling on a shotgun is an unusual sight in this country, although more popular in Europe, but it can be an advantage in waterfowling. It should be easily detachable, since it is removed when you're in the blind and attached for carrying. I prefer to use a gun case with a shoulder strap, which gives protection for the gun as well as ease of carrying. Let me advise against fleece-lined cases for this purpose, however. Once wet, they tend to retain moisture and are hard to dry.

Most of us won't take along a repair kit for hip boots or waders, although there have been times I regretted that, but there is a new item worth sticking in the shell bucket. It's called Miracle-Patch, a small stick of space-age adhesive which can be used on cloth, plastic or rubber. One end of the stick is heated with match or lighter until it begins to flow, then it is applied to the damaged area.

Hand warmers are great gadgets to help keep you warm. About the size of a cigarette case (or twice that with the big models), they're powered by liquid fuel (good lighter fluid will work) or by solid fuel sticks.

Some gunners swear by electric socks for keeping the feet warm, and small, efficient catalytic heaters are now available which are great for boat, pit or blind. Some of the latter operate from propane tanks and some from liquid fuel. Many a duck or goose hunter has warmed himself over a charcoal bucket.

A duck carrier is a very handy item. This is a leather strap with a number of strips at each end which can be slipped over the head of a duck or goose, the whole thing then being balanced on your shoulder.

Use caution around water, and make sure you have a life

A duck strap is a very handy item if ducks or geese must be carried any distance.

preserver handy when boating across deep water. Duck and goose hunters are usually heavily laden with clothes, boots and shells, which don't increase a man's ability to stay afloat.

If you do much wading in marsh or flooded timber where you might slip into a hole, one of the small inflatables isn't a bad safety measure. One is available which will inflate automatically when it gets wet, and another inflates when you squeeze it.

Take along a pair of binoculars on your hunts, and you'll add tremendously to the pleasure of the outing. Many fine glasses are now available which are both light in weight and quite small.

These 6x or 7x glasses are about the smallest that most people can hold steady, though there are binoculars available which are even smaller and lighter, such as Zeiss' tiny 8x glasses. However, Leitz's larger Trinovids probably set the standards for quality in the industry. These latter glasses are expensive in terms of initial cost, but will last for years. My 10x40 Trinovids (about $300) have performed superbly in a wide range of situations, and they are almost waterproof.

Binoculars are a great aid in duck and goose identification, which is important in this age of species restrictions and point-system bag limits. It's an advantage to recognize what kind of bird it is *before* the flock is in over the decoys.

But identifying and watching waterfowl is only one of the pleasures and benefits of the binoculars. They are invaluable for keeping tabs on dead or crippled ducks which float or swim away . . . for watching the activity at other blinds which might be in sight . . . and just for the pleasure of viewing the varied wildlife associated with waterfowl habitat.

The small, portable CB radios (walkie-talkies) have been a source of convenience and pleasure in my waterfowling over the past few years. If wife Mary, sons Tom and Kent, and I are split between blinds within two or three miles of each other, we can keep in touch via the CB's. Under ideal conditions, five- to ten-mile range is possible. It is quite an advantage to be able to coordinate the time of leaving the blinds. Being able to communicate with another blind, or with the outside world, has obvious safety advantages, too. The little 5-watters weigh only a couple of pounds apiece, and can be bought for less than $100 each.

You may find very useful a bag which Orvis markets under the name of "Watertight Camera Bag and Stuff Bag." It is especially good for cameras or other gear you must protect from water. Air, trapped inside the bag when you seal it, will float the bag in case of capsizing. There are two sizes, 11x15 inches and 14x24 inches.

Tips

No matter how high your boots—short, hip, waist or chest waders—there will be times when you'll go too deep. You'll take that one more step when better judgment indicates otherwise, or you'll stumble and fall, or the pirogue will tip over.

The quicker you can get the water out of your footgear the better off you'll be. If you've taken along an extra pair of dry stockings, you'll bless yourself for the foresight.

Back at camp your chore will be to dry the boots before the next day's hunt. Turn hip boots and waders inside out as much as possible, and then hang them *upside down* near some source of heat. Heat rises, of course, which is the reason for this elementary move.

Stuffing crumpled newspapers inside boots will absorb excess moisture, but replace the wet paper regularly. One very good gimmick is to use a hair dryer to dry your boots, since the hot air circulating around in them will do the job faster and better than anything else. Also satisfactory are the electrical dryers made especially for the purpose. Whatever you do, use care, since too much heat can damage rubber.

Thermos jugs. Where weight isn't a problem, you'll be ahead of the game if you buy the stainless-steel kind. They are more expensive but are unbreakable, and the attrition on glass thermos inserts in duck blind or goose pit is ferocious. Just one experience of unscrewing the thermos top on a bitter cold morning, expecting a stimulating shot of hot coffee, and finding instead a broken insert ... well, that will convince most that the stainless-steel is worth the money.

Mail-order catalog houses

Burnham Brothers, P.O. Box 100C, Marble Falls, Tex. 78654
Eddie Bauer, P.O. Box 3700, Seattle, Wash. 98124
Bob Hinman Outfitters, 1217 W. Glen, Peoria, Ill. 61614
Gander Mountain, P.O. Box 248, Wilmot, Wis. 53192
Hunting World, 16 East 53rd St., New York, N.Y. 10022
L. L. Bean, Inc., Freeport, Maine 04032
Orvis, Manchester, Vermont 05254

Chapter 13

Film It

REMEMBER THAT GORGEOUS sunrise on opening day last fall? First there was a faint tinge of light in the east, just about the time the night creatures were giving way to the day shift, and almost before you knew it that red ball of fire edged up over the horizon. What a sight! With that steady stream of geese in silhouette against that brightening sky.

Whap! Man, you sure smoked that lone teal that slipped in from behind and almost got by us. And you made quite a picture yourself, wading back in with that little fellow.

How could you ever forget that guide who handled your sneakbox up on Merrymeeting Bay? He was a real old-timer,

Pictures prolong the pleasure of hunting trips, and the cameras and films available today make them easy to get. Don't be afraid to try unusual shots such as this dawn silhouette scene.

a great character, and didn't he know his duck shooting! Had a mustache, didn't he? Or was it just a beard? And that was some old Parker he was shooting. Or was it a Model 12?

What a shoot we had! I've never seen ducks work as well as they did that day for everybody. Yep, that was in 1952 . . . see, it's written right here on the back of this picture. Look at George, clowning with that mallard. He did have to do *some* shooting before finishing his limit. That was a good bunch of guys. There's Jack, Lewis, Paul, and Jack's guest—Evans, don't remember his first name—and you. I took the picture. Should have had you take one of me.

Memories. The clarity of "unforgettable" events has a way of dimming over the years, unless aided by a pictorial record.

Photography has become the great American obsession. A tourist isn't a tourist unless he has a camera around his neck or in his hands, and that applies to outdoor vacationists as much, or more so. But let's face it, next best to being on lake or marsh participating in the sport of waterfowling itself is reliving those hours in bull sessions around camp, den or living room. The reliving is much more graphic and enjoyable if you have pictures of those days afield.

Waterfowlers, for some reason, lag behind fishermen and campers and even hunters of other game in capturing their activity on film. Perhaps it's the aquatic nature of much of their sport, and the probability of bad weather on many occasions, that mitigate against more gunners taking their cameras with them. They're missing a lot.

There once was a time when good cameras were so complicated that many hunters just didn't want to make the effort, to divert that much time and thought away from the primary goal of duck and goose hunting. No longer is that true. Now you can have a good camera that is simple to use too. Now there is just no excuse for not picturing your gunning for future pleasure.

What kind of camera?

Many hunters are totally confused when they walk into a camera store to "shop." The array of models is staggering. Do they want prints or slides, negative color or transparencies? Single-lens reflex, twin-lens reflex, rangefinder 35mm, half-frame 35mm, Instamatic, Polaroid, interchangeable-lens capability, miniature 35mm, electronic shutter, built-in meter, pocket camera . . .

You can buy a 35mm camera for less than $50 or more than $500, an Instamatic from $20 to $200. The choice is endless.

Most waterfowlers will want their finished product in the form of prints—pictures that they can look at, put into an album, and send copies of to friends. They don't want to make a federal case out of their photography, nor to spend a bundle of money on equipment or a batch of time learning how to take pictures.

Within those parameters we can make a couple of recommendations which should fit the needs of a majority of the duck and goose hunters who need help in their selection. "Instamatic" and "Pocket Camera" are the magic words.

Kodak spawned the idea of a cartridge-loading still camera (as opposed to a movie camera) more than five years ago, and it was a monumental breakthrough in simplicity and efficiency. To load one all you do is open the back, drop in a cartridge, and close the back. No fussing or threading. They were an "instant" success, and still are.

The low end of the Instamatic line sells in the $15 to $25 range, and produces acceptable pictures. As you move up the line the models have better lenses and more features, cost more, and produce better pictures. The top of the line can cost you $150 to $200 and more.

All of the Instamatics have automatic exposure control,

which means that your light setting will be correct with no effort on your part. At the low end of the line the cameras are fixed-focus, and the combination of fixed focus and automatic exposure control means that all you need do is point and push the trigger.

Fixed focus means that everything from four or five feet on out is approximately in focus. The great depth of field of these cameras produces acceptable prints over this wide focus range. The better Instamatics do have a focus control, a very simple split-image affair which is easy to use and which gives more precise focusing, and hence sharper prints.

Several other manufacturers now have similar cartridge-loading cameras designed for Kodak's 126 film cartridges, so you have a choice of more than one brand name.

In 1972, Kodak unveiled a new line of Instamatic "Pocket Cameras." This is a series of five one-inch-thick, cartridge-loading cameras which are the ultimate in portability. Even with smaller film, these Pocket Cameras produce even better pictures.

These cameras are flat, so they fit into a pocket with ease. They have no exposure settings, having an electronic shutter and/or an automatic aperture system. The two modestly priced models—20 and 30—are fixed-focus from 5 feet to infinity. Model 40 has two-position focus, one 3 to 6 feet, and the other beyond 6 feet. Models 50 and 60 can be focused from 3 feet out to infinity.

I doubt that the average waterfowler could go wrong in picking either the regular Instamatic or the Pocket Camera to record his days afield. Choose the model to fit your needs and your pocketbook. The new Pocket Cameras range from $30 up to $138.

With either line of these Instamatics your film choice includes Kodacolor, which is best for color prints; Ektachrome and Kodachrome, which are best for color slides to be viewed with a projector and screen; and Verichrome Pan, for black-

The greatest discipline of all, for a photographer, is to take pictures when the birds are coming in, when the action is taking place.

and-white prints. No matter what type of film you're using, when you drop the cartridge in your camera your exposure control is automatically set for that particular film.

All of these Instamatics accept flash cubes for night pictures, or for a fill light even in the daytime.

One other unconventional camera deserves particular mention, and that's the picture-in-a-minute Polaroid. This amazing invention has caught the fancy of the public as few things have, and it has great potential for the outdoorsman.

One disadvantage to the Polaroid is that it is rather large and bulky, which makes it impractical for taking to the blind or pit in many situations. Where this isn't true you can get some great shots right there on the scene, and see your results immediately.

Whether you take the Polaroid to the blind or not, you can have it in the auto or in camp for those after-the-hunt pictures. Although you get no negative, you can easily get copies of your prints from the Polaroid Copy Service.

It's the nature of the animal that you are left with a good bit of paper trash after taking Polaroid pictures. Make sure you leave none of it lying around. Dispose of it properly.

Okay, there you have my recommendations for a camera for most waterfowlers, who just want pictures to document their hunt. But that doesn't mean that there aren't dozens of other cameras which won't do as well or better in capable hands.

If you want to move up the scale a bit, to full 35mm size, you have hundreds of options. This size is ideal for slide transparencies, but you can also go to negative color film (Kodacolor or Ektacolor), which is best for color prints.

One 35mm which has a lot going for it is the Electro-35 by Yashica. It has an electronic shutter which does all of your exposure adjusting, plus an array of other aids to make sure you get good pictures. Another excellent full-frame 35mm is the tiny Rollei 35, which has a sharp lens and a built-in exposure meter.

Moving on up in 35mm, the top professional lines are the Pentax, Canon, Nikon and Leica, listed approximately in ascending order of price. All are excellent for the serious photographer.

If you really become interested in photography—and well you might—get a good book on photography. There are a number of good ones on the market.

What to shoot

As long as you have that camera along, ready for action, you'll think of things to shoot. The main point is simple. Go ahead and take pictures. Exposing a roll on a hunt is a modest investment in future pleasures.

You may hear criticism now and then of pictures which show the hunters with their game, but those photos have a place. Go ahead and take your buddies with their limits of ducks or geese, or their one or two ducks, their skunked expressions. All serve a purpose, a reminder in years to come of just how that particular hunt went.

Don't neglect the candid and the semi-candid situations: putting out the decoys, a shot of the blind and the boat, the retriever bringing one in. Try an action photo now and then, of birds decoying, hanging over the blocks, if you can keep from grabbing your shotgun.

Scenes around the camp have provided me with some of my favorite waterfowling photographs. I recall one of everybody picking ducks, and another of Mr. Campbell making that great duck gumbo, and one of Mary cooking breakfast at some ungodly hour in the goose camp. And that dandy of Andy Devine and his wife, Doagie, Mary and me, with the

You'll get a few complaints from your hunting buddies if you're taking pictures while the work is going on, but recording such events as putting decoys together is worth the effort, and really doesn't take much time.

It isn't just the big moments which make for memories; also try to capture the little vignettes which add so much to an outing.

solitary goose the four of us killed in a whole day of gunning. Memories.

Closeups are the pictures which really tell the story, while the medium and the long shots set the scene. Don't neglect to move in tight, to the inner limits of focusing on your camera, for those "portrait" photographs of your buddy blowing his duck call and that Lab carrying a duck.

Take care

The cameras listed above are pretty rugged instruments, but they still require protection from hard knocks, dust and dirt,

PHOTO BY DONALD HANSON, COURTESY ORVIS CO.

Caring for cameras and film requires special effort in many duck and goose hunting situations. Protecting them from water is the primary concern, and waterproof bags such as these (available from some mail-order houses and camera stores) are one answer.

and water. There are a number of easy ways to provide such protection.

If you carry the camera in your pocket, and it isn't in a case, slip it into a plastic "baggie" first. That will protect it from dust, dirt and/or tobacco crumbs which might be in that pocket, none of which help the smooth operation of a camera nor the resolving ability of a lens.

Keep the lens clean. A soft, lint-free cotton handkerchief is okay for cleaning the lens (who has lens-cleaning tissue in a duck blind?), but first blow the lens free of most dust and all grit. If you don't, that dust and grit will scratch the lens.

If you carry your camera in a shell bucket, or anywhere

else it may be subjected to bumps and knocks, here's a good trick. Wrap it in a piece of plastic foam and slip a rubber band or two around it. That gives great protection. Put the camera in a plastic baggie first, of course, to cope with the dust and moisture.

Foam insulation material, used widely as the padding in cushions, is available in most discount, department and specialty stores. A thickness of half an inch to an inch is about right for wrapping around a camera.

Be prepared to keep your camera from getting soaked. If you have a shell bucket or waterproof duffle bag in the blind, no problem. If not—or as an alternate solution—take along a heavy waterproof plastic bag in which you can wrap the camera. The usual "baggie" isn't strong enough for this purpose, but a "garbage" bag usually is. Waterproof nylon bags, with drawstrings, are available in many sizes from the mail-order houses.

Don't subject your film, in or out of the camera, to intense heat. That's not usually a problem during the waterfowl season, but in some areas it could be.

The auto glove compartment is probably responsible for the loss of more film than any other single cause. It is like an oven even in moderately warm weather, and is no place for camera or film. Much of its big toll results from this pattern of activity: the sportsman shoots half a roll of film on a trip, tosses the camera into the glove compartment, and forgets it for several months.

Have that film developed as soon as possible after it's exposed, even if you "lose" the part of the roll you didn't shoot. That's far better than losing the entire roll, especially those irreplaceable images of a hunting trip.

Chapter 14

Waterfowl Management

THE TWO PRIMARY activities of waterfowl management are preservation and restoration of habitat, and establishing the hunting regulations each year. Both are essential to the continued well-being of this resource.

Ducks and geese are creatures of wetlands, which makes it imperative that we ensure the continued existence of that kind of habitat. We will discuss this aspect in detail in the following three chapters. Here we will concentrate on how the regulations are set, and on other aspects of management.

Flyways

For the purpose of administrative management, the United

States is divided into four waterfowl flyways: Atlantic, Mississippi, Central and Pacific. These are arbitrary delineations, with boundaries sometimes dividing states, and are an effort to regulate the gun pressure and waterfowl harvest of states in accord with the bird populations and reproductive success of the nesting grounds which supply ducks and geese to those areas.

Setting season lengths and bag limits which will permit the maximum amount of gunning recreation commensurate with the continued well-being of waterfowl is a complex affair. These regulations are now a product of the U.S. Bureau of Sport Fisheries and Wildlife, since migratory birds are the jurisdictional responsibility of the federal government, but it was not always so. It was not until 1913 that Congress passed an act to assume this control.

The flyway concept permits the setting of different regulations in each, but present-day management includes additional variations for certain states and for individual areas within states. The goal is more precise management of the resource.

Although the flyway concept may be the best which has been devised for management purposes, the flyway corridors are not as precise as many sportsmen imagine. States which border on flyway lines, of course, will understandably welcome birds which funnel down the adjacent flyway. But quite apart from the juxtaposition, certain segments of the waterfowl population migrate in strange fashion.

A classic case is that of the canvasback. From prime Manitoba nesting grounds the bulk of these great birds move into Minnesota, thence to Wisconsin, Michigan, and on to wintering grounds of Chesapeake Bay, on the Atlantic coast. There are many other examples.

Despite the variations from the pattern of north to south migrations, waterfowl managers have been able to do a fairly good job of distributing kill in accord with abundance. In the past quarter-century a vast amount of data have been accumulated by the Bureau, the states, Canadian governmental organizations and by Ducks Unlimited, to the point where we can now pinpoint with reasonable certainty the origin of most wintering duck and goose populations.

The banding of waterfowl has added tremendously to our knowledge of migration patterns and to waterfowl mortality rates. This duck is being banded by a U.S. agent in Saskatchewan.

With that accomplished (largely through banding), managers were in a position to make annual surveys of duck and goose reproductive success. Using that data, a forecast of the magnitude of the flight which would migrate south from each production area, and keying it to the estimated gun pressure along the migratory routes each species follows, they recommend seasons and bag limits.

That is essentially the procedure followed each year by the Bureau of Sport Fisheries and Wildlife. Periodic surveys by air and from the ground, conducted on the breeding grounds during the summer, record the condition of the habitat, the nesting success, and the trend of the total breeding popula-

PHOTO BY REX GARY SCHMIDT,
COURTESY BUREAU OF SPORT FISHERIES AND WILDLIFE

Preservation and restoration of wetlands is the most vital phase of waterfowl management, for without them the resource will vanish. However, a key tool is the annual survey on the breeding grounds made by the Bureau of Sport Fisheries and Wildlife, to determine the relative size of the nesting population and the success of the nesting season, for seasons and limits are based on this survey.

tion. From those figures a determination is made as to the seasons and bag limits which are appropriate for various regions of the nation.

Surveying is not an exact science, and there are flaws in the system. Time, money and personnel limit the intensiveness and scope of the surveys, but as of now they provide the best information available. Although some key administrators in the Bureau lean heavily toward the conservative, which perhaps is understandable, there have been significant and encouraging innovations in the past decade designed to utilize the waterfowl resource more fully within the bounds of sound management.

Controlling the harvest is done through a great many restrictions, some of which modern hunters now take for granted. Among the first such placed into effect was an end to spring and summer shooting, which few would now dream of doing. Market hunting, the selling of waterfowl, was ended. Shooting hours, live decoys, the three-shot-capacity limitation, baiting, shooting from motorboats—all are provisions which to many of us have always been part of the gunning picture, when in fact all are of recent origin.

Seasons and bag limits, therefore, constitute only two of many provisions designed to prevent overshooting.

Species management

The goal of individual regulations on certain species is to prevent overgunning of those in short supply, and to permit additional harvest of those in good supply. In the first decades of species management, it was limited solely to what *not* to shoot, but in recent years the concept has been expanded to more fully utilize the potential of this management tool.

For species management to work, of course, the gunner

must be able to identify birds before he shoots. That places
a premium upon waterfowlers' ability and willingness to become competent at doing just that, but the rewards of the
system are worth it.

One "don't shoot" rule which was in effect nationwide for
the 1972–73 season was for canvasbacks. For several years
prior to that there had been a daily limit of one can, which
most hunters considered as an in-case-you-make-a-mistake al-
lowance, but even that has not curbed the continued decline
of canvasback populations. That decline has been a puzzling
one, continuing even when habitat conditions on the nesting
grounds was good and gun pressure on the species low.

Redheads enjoyed the same kind of protection in the three
eastern flyways, for the same reason. The general regulations
on wood ducks specify no more than two per day in the bag
limit. With geese the limit is so many of these species, or group
of species, per day.

Liberalizing limits via species regulations came in the form
of bonus ducks. In addition to a regular daily limit, a hunter
could shoot additional birds provided they were of the right
species. Scaup and teal are two species permitted as bonus
in some areas in recent years, but more than two decades ago
some daily limit regulations ended with "provided that X
number of the birds are mallards."

It is a move in the right direction. The hunter is required
to identify prohibited species or be penalized, but he is permitted more liberal limits if he can identify and shoot bonus
ducks.

In the past few years species management, however, has
moved substantially beyond that point with a "point-system"
bag limit. Duck species *and sexes* are assigned certain point
values, and the daily limit of a hunter has been reached when
the total point values of the ducks he has taken reaches or
exceeds 100. That total, of course, could be altered as conditions dictate in coming years, but the "100" has been in effect
during the experimental seasons just past.

Note that a new ingredient has been added. Selective shooting of males and females, a key feature of deer and pheasant management, now enters the picture. The goal here is to permit greater harvest of male ducks, which have a lower natural mortality than do females, and to conserve the females upon which productivity so greatly depends.

This distinction as to sex won't work with all species. Male and female geese look alike, and so do some ducks such as the black duck and mottled duck. With other duck species there is a difference, but the physical appearance is not sufficiently apparent with ducks on the wing to be of practical value. The sex differential in limit regulations, therefore, has until now been applied only to mallards and pintails.

Under the point system in effect in fourteen states during the 1972–73 season, here are the point values assigned for various species and sexes: 90-point ducks—wood duck, hen mallard, and hooded merganser; 20-point ducks—drake mallard, hen pintail, ring-necked duck; 10-point ducks—all other species and sexes, with exceptions.

Black ducks are 90-point ducks in Mississippi and Atlantic flyways, but 20-pointers in certain Central and Pacific states. The greenwing teal is a 20-pointer in Florida and New Jersey, but only a 10-pointer elsewhere.

In most of the point-system states, it is apparent from the above, a "limit" could vary widely. It could be ten drake pintails, or ten teal, scaup, gadwall, baldpate or shoveler. Or five drake mallards or hen pintails. Or two hen mallards or wood ducks.

The sequence of shooting can play a significant part in a "limit" bag under the point system. That limit could contain one hen mallard but be a limit of ten birds, if the mallard were the last duck killed. Or it could be a limit of two birds, if that mallard were one of the first two shot.

Despite the probability that some hunters have, do and will "rearrange" the order of killing of their ducks in order to increase their allowable daily limit, all evidence thus far indicates that the point system is a success. The average kill under it, in fact, is slightly less than the comparable average kill under fixed limits.

It has also been successful, according to the analysis of the data thus far, in diverting gun pressure from ducks in short supply and toward those in good supply.

If you simply cannot learn to identify ducks on the wing, or aren't willing to make the effort, the point system has a built-in provision to take care of you. (You must still be able to avoid shooting prohibited species, on which there is a total closure, but that is true no matter what bag-limit system is in effect.) Just go ahead and kill any legal duck which comes in and *then* identify it, which you *must* be able to do. If it's a 90-pointer, you know that the next duck you shoot, whatever the species or sex, completes your daily limit. Just tally your points as they hit the water, and pick up your decoys when the total reaches or exceeds 100.

Point of diminishing return

When waterfowl populations decrease, the obvious move is to reduce the loss by hunting via a curtailment on the length of the open season and a reduction in the bag limit. It is a sound, useful management technique, especially since gun pressure seems to play a greater role in annual mortality of waterfowl than it does on such other game species as quail, doves, rabbits and squirrels.

It should be kept in mind, however, that one of the greatest forces for the continued well-being of waterfowl is the hunter. A relatively small segment of the shooting public, numbering something over two million, it performs all out of proportion to its numbers.

Waterfowlers are the greatest force agitating for the salvation of what wetlands remain and for the restoration of what we have lost. As the next chapter, on Ducks Unlimited, will

Complete closure of a waterfowl season, or even severe restriction of it, should not be undertaken lightly, since it could do more harm than good insofar as ducks and geese are concerned. When the bag limit dropped to two ducks per day in the Mississippi Flyway several years ago, many duck clubs decided not to operate. Winter duck habitat suffered, since many rice fields and timber stands weren't flooded.

relate, they have voluntarily contributed many millions of dollars via DU for wetlands work in Canada. And many millions more via "duck stamp" fees to the federal government for a variety of conservation purposes. And more millions through an 11 percent excise tax on sporting arms and ammunition, which goes to the states through the Bureau of Sport Fisheries and Wildlife under the Pittman-Robertson program.

Private duck-hunting clubs throughout the United States and Canada have been responsible for the preservation of millions of acres of wetlands. Marshes, which long ago would have been drained and put to some other use, had they not been desirable for duck hunting, remain an immensely valuable part of our aquatic heritage which benefit a vast number of creatures.

Curtailment of duck and goose hunting opportunities can reach a point of diminishing return if it drives from the ranks of waterfowlers a significant portion of this potent force. If such restrictions result in the draining of thousands of acres of wetlands, then the price of saving ducks from hunter harvest may have been too high. Season and bag-limit regulations must always play a vital role in the management of our waterfowl resources, but federal officials should constantly keep in mind the consequences of tipping the balance too far in the other direction.

If the hunting season in any flyway is ever completely closed, as was recommended by some officials in the early 1960's for the Mississippi Flyway, it is my considered opinion that the waterfowl habitat and the resource itself will suffer a grievous loss. The history of complete closures on federally controlled species is one of extreme reluctance to reopen them again. It would not take many such years to drive from the scene the duck clubs which now maintain so much vital habitat.

One year, for many, would be sufficient. Then, when and if the duck season ever reopened, permanent pastures, soybeans and housing developments would have replaced those marshes.

Shortstopping

The migratory instinct of waterfowl to fly south in the winter is well known, but the degree of that instinct and the distance traveled varies tremendously. Some zip right out of this country to winter in South America, while others have traditionally wintered as far north as Illinois.

That migratory instinct, especially of birds which remain in this country, can be thwarted, and that has happened to

For years it was believed that blue and snow geese were immune to shortstopping, but those which formerly overflew the Midwest enroute to Texas and Louisiana are spending more and more time in Missouri and Kansas. The well-being of the birds themselves would be better served if they wintered over the huge expanse of marshes along the Gulf Coast than if they are jammed into small refuge concentrations in the Midwest, where disease could decimate the flock very quickly.

a substantial degree in the past two decades. Some of the "shortstopping," as the phenomena of waterfowl stopping short of their traditional wintering grounds has come to be called, is attributed to changes in land-use practices, and as such were unforeseen and unintentional. Other instances have been by design, a program geared specifically toward encouraging birds to remain farther north than would normally be the case.

The Canada goose is the classic case in point. In the Mississippi Valley the historic wintering grounds of this majestic bird was centered in the lower portion of the flyway, with tens of thousands of them reaching the Gulf Coast of Louisiana. In 1927 the state of Illinois made a move which was the beginning of the end of honker flocks as far as the bottom end of the flyway is concerned. The move was to buy 3,500 acres of bottomland in southern Illinois to form the Horseshoe Lake Refuge.

Illinois waterfowl specialists decided that offering food and protection might influence geese to stay in that state longer, so corn, wheat and grass were planted on the refuge. The plan worked, and then some, until half of the Canada goose population of the Mississippi Valley—some 200,000 birds—were wintering in this one area. Few ever went farther south.

It was a bonanza for hunters of that area and for the small town of Cairo, which quickly became the "goose capital" of the nation. Hunting clubs sprang up all around the tiny refuge, and took a fearful toll when the hungry Canadas, having eaten all of the food planted on the refuge, ranged across the boundaries to forage in the surrounding fields.

The semi-domesticated geese were no match for the ring of goose pits, one after another in successive circles outside the refuge, and the kill soared. In 1945, hunters killed 5,000 geese in five days, spurring authorities to close the season.

A year or two later the federal government took over the 45,000-acre Crab Orchard National Wildlife Refuge, and there began to produce several thousand acres of grain and pasture each year. The goal, ostensibly, was to disperse the Horseshoe Lake flock, but the dispersal couldn't be very great since the two refuges are only 50 miles apart.

But the Crab Orchard flock of Canada geese rose from zero in 1947 to 48,000 in 1953.

The shortstopping, however, didn't end at the Illinois level. In 1941 the U.S. Fish and Wildlife Service bought a 21,000-acre refuge in Wisconsin and began to plant cereal crops in a special effort to attract geese. In 1949 it drew 10,000 geese, and two years later an amazing 100,000. Three thousand acres of corn, wheat and small grains was the attraction, coupled with the protection of the refuge.

The state of Wisconsin got into the act by buying another 10,000 acres on the south end of this Horicon National Wildlife Refuge, and the hunting kill went out of sight. In 1958 some 15,000 geese were killed around Horicon, and the next year 25,000. Now Wisconsin was shortstopping geese from Illinois, and 90 percent of the entire Mississippi Valley goose population was wintering on these two areas.

The huge kill finally resulted in harvest quotas being set for the Horicon area and for the Horseshoe Lake area. For the 1972–73 season, the quotas were fixed at 28,000 for Wisconsin and 28,000 for Illinois.

Meanwhile, the migration of Canada geese to the southern end of the flyway had come to an end, and the seasons in Arkansas and Louisiana closed completely. Not only did this mark the end of a grand era in waterfowling in North America, but it was (and is) at the expense of transforming a splendid, wary bird into a hand-fed, semi-domesticated ward of state and federal government.

By 1960 the huge Canada goose flock at Horicon Refuge had become a major tourist attraction. Traffic problems on State Highway 49, which crosses east-west across the refuge, were so severe that the state finally built two miles of wide parking space on either side of the highway. As George Laycock put it, in his fine book *The Sign of the Flying Goose*, "Here, visitors can sometimes see as many as 30,000 Canada geese, some feeding at a distance of 30 yards."

That last epitomizes the demise of a bird once known as the wariest of them all. There yet remain segments of the Canada-goose population, in the west and in the east, which have not yet succumbed to the welfare state.

Federal, state and private refuges and shooting grounds in Missouri completed the shortstopping of Canada populations which formerly migrated down the Mississippi Flyway. Along the East Coast, sanctuary-shooting grounds in Maryland and Delaware have begun drying up the migrations of Canadas which once wintered at Matamuskeet in North Carolina.

The shortstopping practices have opened up a Pandora's box of ills, along with the benefits to hunters and to bird watchers in the areas of the concentrations. Although a modest amount of "slowing" the migrations would obviously be of benefit to some areas of the nation, the movement has snowballed beyond the ability of federal and state agencies to control it.

The Bureau of Sport Fisheries and Wildlife, with whom the ultimate responsibility lies, has given lip service but little more to coping with the problem over two decades. It was unwilling to make the drastic moves which might have been successful in encouraging Canada geese to resume their traditional migration patterns, and now it is doubtful if anything could accomplish that goal.

Many wildlife administrators and biologists, including the noted conservationists on the Committee on Bird Protection of the American Ornithologists Union, have warned for more than a decade of the dangers which were developing: "These artificial concentrations," said the above committee, "could endanger the security of certain races and segments of the goose population."

Dispersal over wide areas is the protective mantle for virtually all wildlife species, yet the artificially provided food and sanctuary of the refuges in question are accomplishing exactly the opposite. They concentrate geese in staggering numbers on incredibly small areas, making such flocks vulnerable to gun pressure and disease.

So much for the Canada goose. How about the blues and snows? The traditional migration pattern of these in the Mississippi and Central flyways was largely one of overflight from Canada to the coasts of Louisiana and Texas. Stops enroute for appreciable segments were rare and of short duration, but these birds are also being shortstopped in huge numbers. The Bureau, once again, seems to be completely unwilling or unable to cope with a repeat of the Canada goose debacle.

Shortstopping of the blues and snows is almost wholly by design. As one Bureau official put it: "There has been growing concern over the migrational behavior of that portion of the continental blue/snow goose population which winters primarily in Louisiana and Texas. Some observers contend that a large segment of this population is abandoning its ancestral wintering grounds and are wintering farther north, specifically in Kansas and Missouri. . . . In the past, goose management has consisted of planting the appropriate foods, providing sufficient marsh roosts in a sanctuary and hoping eventually to attract large numbers of geese. This was successful at all three [federal] refuges." The refuges he spoke of are Sand Lake National Wildlife Refuge, South Dakota; Desoto Bend National Wildlife Refuge in Iowa; and Squaw Creek National Wildlife Refuge in Missouri.

A Louisiana wildlife administrator-biologist, commenting on the Bureau management of these three refuges, said: " . . . as a result of [Bureau] efforts, hunting has been concentrated around three federal refuges. This exactly duplicates the Bureau mismanagement of the Canada goose resource. . . . During the past year over 500,000 geese out of the entire flock of 1,300,000 (blues and snows) were held north of their traditional wintering grounds in Louisiana and Texas."

Without drastic action to counter the Bureau policies, that Louisiana official forecast that his state faced "the total shortstopping of blue and snow geese as we were forced to accept the loss of our Canada geese twenty years ago."

With the Bureau showing the way on federal refuges, both state and private areas have plunged into the program of holding blues and snows, and with outstanding "success." It's impossible to fault state or private operators from endeavoring to improve the gunning opportunities for hunters, but the shortstopping is rapidly curtailing and ending shooting farther south.

More important, the well-being of the geese themselves is being ignored in this management program.

Although state officials and hunters in the southern flyway states have been concerned about loss of hunting opportunity, they have also warned of the potential for disease in the dense goose concentrations on refuges farther north. In 1973 that fear became a reality, but with ducks rather than geese, when an outbreak of duck viral enteritis took place on the Lake Andes National Wildlife Refuge in South Dakota.

This refuge is only 939 acres in size (300 acres of corn and milo at the time of the outbreak) with 220 acres of water. About 15 acres of water were kept free of ice by a flowing artesian well, and up to 100,000 ducks remained there throughout the winter. It was in this jammed-packed concentration that the first dead birds were discovered on January 8, 1973. Before the end of the month more than twenty thousand dead mallards, and a number of Canada geese, were collected on the Refuge, plus others on the nearby Missouri River. Estimates of the total kill run well over thirty thousand birds lost.

Almost one year prior to the Lake Andes disease outbreak, Dr. Frank A. Hayes of the Southeastern Cooperative Wildlife Disease Study wrote: "When wild or domestic animals are concentrated in abnormally high numbers, the contact index for transmission of infectious diseases is proportionally increased. Because of a semi-aquatic environment, this is especially true with waterfowl, whereas there are many native disease entities capable of inflicting heavy mortality in birds concentrated at levels such as [on the goose refuges in question], e.g. fowl cholera, botulism, parasitism, etc. In the event of certain foreign disease introductions, these circumstances could be disastrous."

Duck viral enteritis, known as Dutch duck plague, is just

such a "foreign disease," unknown in the United States before 1967.

Quite apart from the loss of hunting opportunities to the south which have resulted and will continue to result from the shortstopping, the Bureau has a clear-cut obligation to the geese themselves to correct the problem of overconcentration. The task will not be easy, and will require drastic action, but the problem is largely one of the Bureau's own making.

As witnessed by the Lake Andes incident, mallards are also subject to shortstopping tactics. It should be pointed out, however, that the bulk of the mallard population of the Mississippi Flyway has traditionally wintered north of the Gulf Coast states, with more in Arkansas and Illinois than in Louisiana. The danger with mallards as with geese is that they may be concentrated in tiny refuge areas, rather than allowing them to disperse over the millions of acres in the Louisiana marshes, the prairies and flooded timber bottoms of Arkansas, and the vast expanses of the Illinois River bottomlands.

Shortstopping of goose flocks along the Pacific Flyway has not taken place to any appreciable extent. One exception might be the Canadas in the Columbia Basin, which has experienced a buildup from the numbers which traditionally overwintered there.

It is reasonable to predict, however, that the snow geese which provide tremendous hunting in the Central Valley of California can eventually be stopped to the north. Summer Lake in Oregon and the Klamath–Tule Lake district of northern California could possibly wake one year to discover their snow geese are wintering in Washington. And that their Canada geese no longer visit them each winter.

Graphic proof of the shortstopping along the Atlantic Flyway was presented in 1967 by Dale Crider, of the Florida Game and Fresh Water Fish Commission: "All major Canada goose flocks in the Atlantic Flyway south of Chesapeake Bay have declined recently," he wrote.

The Florida wintering population of Canada geese

dropped from 27,000 in 1956 to 6,000 in 1967. From 1955 to 1967, Virginia's flock decreased from 55,000 to 35,000; and North Carolina's plummeted from 255,000 to 66,000.

The other end of the scale showed the increases. In Maryland the flock grew from 69,000 to 360,000; Delaware, from 3,000 to 83,000; Pennsylvania, from 2,000 to 68,000.

Although the problem of shortstopping has most seriously affected the lower states in the Mississippi Flyway, it should obviously be of great concern to all sections of the nation.

Resident flocks

Largely in an effort to circumvent the loss through shortstopping, some states are now trying to establish resident flocks

Efforts of Louisiana and some other states to establish resident, nonmigratory flocks of Canada geese are meeting with some limited success. Shortstopping of the migration by refuges farther north in the flyway have virtually ended Canada flights into Arkansas, Louisiana and Florida, and severely reduced them in North Carolina.

of Canada geese which are nonmigratory. Ohio has been a leader in this, and by 1970 their flock was producing an estimated 8,000 to 10,000 goslings each year. Those birds, however, are not completely nonmigratory, since band returns show that some are being killed by hunters in Tennessee.

Tennessee, which has been able to shortstop some 80,000 Canadas, most of which overwinter on the Tennessee and Reelfoot national wildlife refuges, is also trying to establish resident flocks. So is Louisiana, which has "enjoyed" a complete closed season on these geese since 1963, although it once wintered more than 100,000 Canadas. In that state—and Arkansas—a resident flock seems to hold the only hope for future gunning.

An artificial place to nest

The wood duck, in addition to holding the crown as the most beautiful of all species, is also the All-American duck, since it nests almost wholly within the contiguous forty-eight states of the United States. It nests throughout the eastern half of the United States and winters along the southern tier of states. It nests and winters, also, along the northwest coastal states.

As the name implies, the wood duck is a creature largely of the wooded lakes, streams and swamps. That, coupled with the extreme beauty of the plumage of the drake, led to the decimation of wood-duck flocks early in this century. The birds were killed for their feathers, to be used in the manufacture of artificial fishing flies, with a single skin bringing $3 to $4. The cutting of timber and the draining of swamps made inroads upon both nesting and living habitat.

In 1918 the season on wood ducks was completely closed both in Canada and the United States, and it was not until 1941 that a single wood duck was again permitted in the bag

Cavities for wood-duck nesting are a limiting factor in some areas, and wood-duck boxes such as this are worthwhile. The collar of aluminum around the tree is to protect the duck eggs and ducklings from predators, largely snakes and raccoons.

of several states. The birds have bounced back, but special bag-limit restrictions are still in effect.

Wood ducks nest in cavities in trees, and a shortage of such holes can be a limiting factor in breeding success. Artificially provided wood-duck boxes have contributed substantially to better production, and involvement in a program of this kind is one of the best projects for sportsmans clubs and youth groups.

Artificial nests and nesting platforms for both Canada geese and mallards also offer promise, with various types affording more safety for the eggs from water fluctuation and from such predators as raccoons and crows. Remington Farms, on the Eastern Shore of Maryland, has done a considerable amount of work along these lines.

Botulism and fowl cholera

Millions of ducks and other aquatic birds have been killed by botulism during the twentieth century. Since it is most prevalent in the Western states, for years it was called "Western Duck Sickness," but now it is known that the malady is a form of botulism.

The first large outbreak of record occurred in the summer of 1910, when millions of aquatic birds died in California and around the Great Salt Lake in Utah. Kills since then have been frequent but erratic, with the loss of an estimated quarter-million ducks on the northern end of the Great Salt Lake in 1932.

This complex disease (more properly, an epidemic) has been found from one coast to the other, and from Mexico to Canada, but it is most frequent in the semi-arid areas of the West. The causative organism, *Clostridium botulinum,* lives in the habitat of the ducks, and its spores germinate and multiply prolifically when conditions are favorable: "suitable temperature, an organic medium to satisfy food requirements, and an absence of atmospheric oxygen," as described by the Bureau of Sport Fisheries and Wildlife.

The actual death of ducks from botulism is caused by respiratory paralysis, which results when they swallow a potent nerve toxin produced by the spores. A rapid fluctuation of the water level of the area involved seems to be the best solution to a botulism outbreak, but in most of the affected areas such a treatment is impossible. In many there is no water available to raise the level of the lake, and in others there is no outlet to permit a rapid drawdown.

An antitoxin is quite effective but requires treatment of individual birds, and in a major outbreak this has limited practical application.

Fowl cholera is an infectious disease of both domestic and wild fowl, and has catastrophic potential for virtually eradicating duck and goose flocks. Overcrowding of susceptible populations, such as is occurring on some federal, state and private areas, particularly in the Midwest but elsewhere as well, favors the spread of such contagious diseases as this one.

Unlike the organism that causes botulism, which is a product of a particular site, fowl cholera may still become a chronic contaminant of concentration areas of waterfowl. The most severe outbreak in recent years took place in the winter of 1956-57 on and around the Muleshoe National Wildlife Refuge in the Texas Panhandle, when more than 60,000 ducks died. A severe outbreak also occurred in 1964 on the Squaw Creek National Wildlife Refuge in Missouri.

There are no really good ways to minimize the effects or to end an epidemic of fowl cholera in ducks or geese, once it begins in a dense concentration of birds. Since the causative organism can exist for at least three months in the decaying flesh of infected birds, an obvious procedure is to collect and burn the carcasses daily, which will minimize the potential for spread to new areas via scavenger birds.

If the lake area is such that it can be increased quickly,

as by filling a lake to capacity or freeing more of a lake from ice, such a measure might have a salutory effect by spreading the waterfowl flock over a wider area, but in most instances this is not possible or practical. And dispersal of the flock, either by draining the lake or permitting it to freeze over, involves the risk of spreading the disease to uncontaminated waters.

The logical course toward helping prevent huge losses is to prevent the buildup of enormous concentrations of ducks and geese on extremely small areas, and to move toward reducing or dispersing those concentrations once they have formed. The Bureau of Sport Fisheries and Wildlife, and the states of the Midwest where such concentrations are annually present, should seriously consider the potential for disaster to those flocks from disease. Such a potential is tremendously

An excellent management-hunting technique is to grow milo and millet, then flood the field to proper depth for the ducks after the grain has matured. Although it is legal to manipulate such a crop (cut it and leave it on the ground, for instance) after it matures for dove hunting, it is not legal to do so for waterfowl.

increased by the artificial, abnormal crowding over long periods.

Duck viral enteritis, as mentioned earlier, is another disease that has become a threat in recent years. The first outbreak of this exotic malady took place on Long Island in 1967, when about sixty-five wild black ducks died. Since then this Dutch duck plague, as it is called, has killed wild ducks in small numbers in both the Long Island and the San Francisco Bay areas, but the Lake Andes tragedy in early 1973 was the first major outbreak in the United States.

As the Director of the Bureau put it, "I simply must proceed on the assumption that this is the first major outbreak *and more should be expected.*"

Lead poisoning

Ducks, geese and swans have been killed by shots which missed for decades. It happens when the birds ingest spent lead pellets with their intake of food and grit. Only a few such pellets can cause the death of a mallard or other species from lead poisoning.

An estimated two to three million waterfowl are lost annually to lead poisoning, making it a significant source of mortality. The problem is acute only in certain areas which have been heavily gunned for decades, and where the habitat is such that the lead shot accumulate and remain available to ducks and geese, but in such areas losses can be severe.

A recent instance was the loss of more than six thousand Canada geese in Maryland and Delaware in early 1972, but the severity of the problem was suspected way back in 1930. It was confirmed in 1939–40 when twelve thousand ducks died of lead poisoning at Herons Lake, Minnesota. A study of thirty-six other lakes revealed widespread occurrence of spent shot in feeding areas, with the pellets remaining available to waterfowl for years.

Catahoula Lake in central Louisiana, one of the most important wintering spots in the Mississippi Flyway, has suffered from periodic outbreaks of lead poisoning for years. A hard-pan clay bottom which prevents shot pellets from sinking into the mud, plus a situation where free-ranging hogs root the bottom of the shallow lake for chufa, combine to make Catahoula a potential hotspot for lead poisoning.

The vast marshes along the coasts of Louisiana and Texas, by contrast, apparently suffer from no lead poisoning at all. The explanation is primarily that the marsh mud is such that the shot sinks and becomes unavailable to waterfowl, and secondarily that the gunning is spread over millions of acres rather than being concentrated over smaller areas.

A search for a substitute for lead shot which would be nontoxic has been under way for years, increasing in intensity

The hard bottom of Catahoula Lake, in Louisiana, makes it possible to drive special vehicles far offshore to blinds, but also makes for a lead-poisoning problem, by preventing the pellets from sinking into the mud.

during the past decade. Various alloys and coatings have been tried, but none met the tests. The task of finding a nontoxic substitute that has a ballistic coefficient suitable for shot and that will not injure gun barrels has been a difficult one.

Soft-iron shot is the most promising thus far, and in the fall of 1972 it was used experimentally by hunters on seven federally controlled hunting areas. A report from the Bureau says that the hunters "found the shells comparable to lead-shot ammunition," which is somewhat in conflict with other experimental tests.

Earlier trials at Pautuxent showed that shells loaded with No. 4 iron shot have almost identical "killing effectiveness" as comparable lead shot loads at shots not exceeding 50 yards. Other tests indicated the comparable effective range at no more than 40 yards, with increased crippling losses beyond that point.

Winchester, Remington and Federal ammunition manufacturers are all involved in research and experiments along the iron-shot line, and it seems that progress is being made toward a reasonable substitute for lead shot in waterfowl hunting. With millions of pounds of lead shot being deposited in hunting areas each year, it is important that the problem be solved.

In February 1973 the Director of the Bureau stated as the goal of that organization: "For the 1973–74 hunting season, the use of iron shot will be expanded to the degree permitted by available supplies of ammunition. Mandatory use of iron shot throughout one flyway will be the aim of the program for the 1974–75 season. Unless ongoing tests turn up unexpected technological problems the Service hopes to recommend regulations imposing a nationwide ban on the use of lead shot for the 1975–76 waterfowl season."

Suggestions have been made that the use of iron shot be made mandatory only in areas of the nation where lead poisoning is known to be a problem, but from the above Bureau release such a plan is apparently not being considered. One

Loss of waterfowl through crippling is of great concern to managers, since it frequently reaches 25 percent of the harvest. Use of retrievers could cut that substantially, but so would a conscientious effort by hunters to make sure their birds are in range before shooting.

facet of the change, according to ammunition manufacturers, is that the cost of shells loaded with soft-iron shot will be substantially greater than for those with lead shot.

Enforcement of any ban on the use of lead shot in waterfowling will be a problem, as is enforcement of many other regulations, but responsible hunters should do everything possible to eliminate unnecessary waste of ducks and geese. Out-of-range skybusting, failure to retrieve dead birds, and loss from lead poisoning and from diseases should all be of grave concern.

Research

The Bureau has an excellent facility for research near Laurel, Maryland, called the Pautuxent Wildlife Research Center, and from it emanates a constant flow of findings which benefit both waterfowl and hunters. Investigations such as those conducted year-round at Pautuxent, and by some state wildlife departments, are essential if huntable waterfowl populations are to be maintained in the coming decades.

Analysis of band returns and bird wings enable workers to determine the hunter harvest of various species, the differential harvest rates of age groups and sexes, and the reproductive success for that particular year. All such data are helpful in the sound management of waterfowl.

Other objects of the researcher's attention are waterfowl losses to pollution, predation, lead poisoning, crippling loss and drainage. They are concerned with ways to increase the breeding productivity of the water areas which we do have, such as the tens of thousands of farm ponds which dot the countryside, and the vast Gulf Coast marshes which are now nesting grounds only for the mottled duck.

In the past some have defined the goal of the Bureau of Sport Fisheries and Wildlife as one of ensuring the perpetuation of ducks, geese and other migratory birds. Not true! As most of the dedicated, competent administrators, biologists and game agents who work for the Bureau will testify, such a goal is too narrow and limited. Beyond that first step of preventing the disappearance of a species, a primary goal of this federal agency—and of all state wildlife departments—should be to improve *hunting* opportunities to the best of its ability commensurate with the well-being of the waterfowl resource.

Chapter 15

Ducks Unlimited

ONE OF THE most stirring dramas in the saga of waterfowl on this continent—indeed, in the saga of outdoor resource conservation throughout the world—is the story of Ducks Unlimited. It is graphic, real-life evidence of the willingness and determination of conservationists in general and of waterfowlers in particular to nurture and preserve a wildlife resource.

Duck and goose hunters and other vitally interested people and organizations have contributed the staggering total of more than $23,000,000 to Ducks Unlimited in the past thirty-five years. It has been an unparalleled outpouring of voluntary contributions to enhance wildlife.

And it has done just that! Almost 80 cents of every dollar contributed—more than $17,000,000—has gone directly into

Canada to plan, build and develop well over a thousand "duck factories," as these projects are called. They encompass some 2,000,000 acres of waterfowl nesting habitat, much of which would surely have passed from existence had it not been for this work.

The DU projects have not only prevented the disappearance of many duck and goose nesting areas, but they have restored a vast number which had already been either partially or completely destroyed in their ability to produce new crops of waterfowl. All of this DU work has been in Canada, since that is where most of our ducks and geese are produced.

DU—symbol of conservation

Of equal importance to the actual marsh restoration and salvation work that Ducks Unlimited has accomplished in Canada, in the eyes of many people, is the role this organization has played in stimulating an awareness of the need for conservation.

On both sides of the border DU has become a symbol, a rally point which focuses the attention of the public upon the urgent need to aid an outdoor resource which is in trouble. This organization has been the cohesive force in developing a working rapport between the Canadian government officials, U.S. government officials, and both Canadian and American hunters and conservationists. In that role its contribution may even be of more importance than the actual construction work done on the nesting grounds.

How it began

The forerunner of Ducks Unlimited was More Game Birds in America, an organization formed in 1929 during a bleak period when waterfowl populations were plunging to record lows. Those men who embarked on this epic undertaking wanted to find the answers to this decrease, and they conducted an intensive study over a period of years to get them.

Among the conclusions resulting from this study were these: (1) Over 65 percent of the continent's waterfowl are produced in three Canadian prairie provinces—Alberta, Saskatchewan and Manitoba. (2) Draining and conversion to cultivated fields, a by-product of the rapid civilization of these areas, was steadily destroying the prime breeding grounds. (3) Natural droughts and floods were becoming increasingly critical as a limiting factor in waterfowl production.

The More Game Birds study concluded that if the duck and geese populations were to be maintained and restored, then immediate efforts must begin toward rehabilitating and preserving the primary nesting areas of Canada. A key word in that conclusion is "Canada."

Thus it was that on January 29, 1937, as an outgrowth of the studies stimulated by More Game Birds in America, a group of American sportsmen incorporated in our nation's capital the organization called Ducks Unlimited. The goal of this unique nonprofit group was, in essence, to raise money in the United States and elsewhere to finance waterfowl habitat preservation and restoration in Canada.

The task which confronted this visionary group was awesome. Both the United States and Canada were in a depression which had lingered for years. The enormousness of the physical task, and the complexity of raising money in one country and spending it in another, would have baffled, discouraged and deterred a less dedicated breed of men, but not that one.

To handle the actual direction and construction of the projects north of the border, a companion Canadian Corporation called Ducks Unlimited (Canada) was formed, under the laws of the Dominion. In that fashion did the first DU wetlands project, Manitoba's Big Grass Marsh, begin in 1938.

The international cooperation in this exciting venture has been truly amazing. Ranchers, landholders, communities and industries have generously granted no-cost, long-term land leases on wetland areas, and the Provincial and Dominion governments of Canada have fostered the movement in innumerable ways. The heart of the progress, of course, has stemmed from the inspiring enthusiasm, dedication and generosity of the American sportsman, and the unselfish direction for the movement provided over the years by DU officers, staff and trustees.

Led by Louisiana, several states now set aside a portion of the income from hunting license sales for use by Ducks Unlimited. In addition to the bayou state, others are Ohio, North Carolina, South Carolina, Arkansas, Wisconsin, and Tennessee.

This is an indication of the value of DU's efforts in Canada in the minds of many U.S. wildlife administrators.

What has DU accomplished?

One of the greatest benefits from DU efforts has been that they have brought to the attention of public and government officials alike the dire necessity for habitat salvation on the Canadian breeding grounds. But what of the physical accomplishments in the expenditure of that $23,000,000 over the past thirty-five years?

Since 1938 Ducks Unlimited has constructed more than 1,200 water-control structures such as dams, dikes and levees. It has under lease almost 2,000,000 acres of prime wetland habitat. The total shoreline, a key factor in duck productivity, measures more than 8,600 miles.

Water is the key to waterfowl productivity. It must be present in the right quantities at the right time in the right place, and it is toward filling these requisites that the Ducks

Ducks Unlimited in action at the large 10,000-acre Cadotte Lake Project, 350 miles northwest of Edmonton, which will provide 54 miles of duck-producing shoreline. Typical of a Ducks Unlimited "northern type" project, the area was developed in cooperation with the Alberta government.

Unlimited construction program is geared. The goal is to prevent the draining of marshes which are already productive, but in addition to provide water control to assure optimum conditions.

These water control projects span the gamut of size, from small units of 50 acres or less to giants of half a million acres. One of the most ambitious ventures ever tackled is now under way near The Pas in Manitoba. This huge Del-Mar Project, called the Mawdesley Wildlife Development, involves 512,000 acres.

Positioning precast slabs on D.U.'s Swedes project, Alberta. Precast structures are valuable time and equipment savers in remote northern areas.

The projects also span Canada. Although most are con-centrated in the "duck factory" Prairie Provinces, others stretch from British Columbia to Nova Scotia and New Brunswick. The production areas of Canada outside the Prairie Provinces are not as productive on a per-acre basis, but their vastness and greater stability from year to year make them extremely important from an overall viewpoint.

But a majority of the ducks killed in the United States are raised in Saskatchewan, Alberta and Manitoba, so let's take a look at those Prairie Provinces. This is pothole country without peer, and a better design for fantastic duck produc-tion couldn't be evolved. In wet years this area has some six to eight *million* potholes, and if they contain water throughout the critical period a great crop of little ducks is produced.

But this is semi-arid country where frequent drought is the rule. About a decade ago there were several years of severe drought back-to-back, and when that occurs the number of those life-producing potholes in these prairie provinces can fall to as low as 600,000.

In this region alone, Ducks Unlimited has created or restored some 600,000 acres of habitat.

A look ahead

It should be noted that the work done by Ducks Unlimited in Canada has had, and is having, benefits reaching far beyond ducks and geese. All creatures which prosper, live and enjoy an aquatic habitat, both birds and animals, have participated in the fruits of the DU endeavors. One reliable estimate tabulated this grouping at some two hundred and fifty species of birds, sixty different mammals and ten types of fish.

In 1970, Ducks Unlimited moved south of the border to form Ducks Unlimited de Mexico, making DU truly international in scope. There Mexican sportsmen are raising funds for waterfowl conservation and management programs in Mexico. It is a significant step, one which should be aided and encouraged, since aquatic habitat there is also under the gun of progress. Many species of ducks and geese which nest in Canada and in the United States either winter in Mexico or pass through it enroute to Central and South America.

Although DU has accomplished an enormous amount of good in the thirty-five years of its existence, it is highly significant and encouraging that recent years have witnessed a mushrooming effectiveness. In 1971, for instance, contributions to DU reached an amazing $3,047,894, an increase in one year of 31.7 percent. Membership zoomed to 65,228—a 31.2 percent increase over the previous year.

There seems little doubt that the momentum of this fine organization is increasing by leaps and bounds, which is very fortunate viewed in the light of the increasing pressures of civilization upon waterfowl living areas—and in the light of the all-out assault on hunting of any kind by certain segments of the public and the media.

The costs of waterfowl habitat salvation and restoration is skyrocketing along with all other costs of doing business, which makes it imperative that income to Ducks Unlimited continue to increase each year.

A tremendously ambitious plan was recently kicked off by DU in cooperation with Canadian governmental agencies, with a completion goal of 1980. One of its key ingredients calls for turning another 4,500,000 acres into drought- and flood-proof duck factories. Each project will be strategically located in a crucial duck-producing area. Varying in size from a few acres to several thousand acres, they should make these areas ideal for waterfowl nesting.

Ducks Unlimited isn't the entire solution to providing a never-ending supply of ducks and geese funneling down the flyways each fall. Substantial, aggressive help, including additional funding, should come from both U.S. and Canadian governments. Many of the "save our birds and animals" groups would be more effective and productive if they devoted a portion of their energies to raising money for DU.

No, DU isn't the total answer, but it is by all odds the best, most productive organization working in behalf of waterfowl and waterfowl hunters in existence. That being the case, there is no better place to invest any surplus dollars you may have. If you value the continued sport of wildfowling enough to have read this far, in fact, a contribution of dollars which aren't really surplus could be the best deposit toward future hunting you could make.

All contributions to DU are deductible for federal income tax purposes. Membership is $10 per year (many give $20 to

$200 or more), which also brings you a subscription to *Ducks Unlimited* magazine. The address is: Ducks Unlimited, Inc., P.O. Box 66300, Chicago, Ill. 60666.

Chapter 16

Dammers & Drainers

WETLANDS!
This one ingredient is *the* one for waterfowl—the make or break factor. Without wetlands there won't be any ducks or geese or any other wildfowl whose habitat is aquatic or semi-aquatic.

At one time this nation was richly blessed with wetlands in enormous quantity and variety, and waterfowl production to match. It is reliably estimated that the United States alone had some 127,000,000 acres of wetland back in those days, but then came man.

Millions of acres of those wetlands have been drained, and waterfowl populations have suffered accordingly. Some of the drainage was necessary in an expanding population; some could have been avoided by sound planning; and much of it was completely unnecessary. Far too much of it, perhaps a majority, was the result of government subsidies with public tax monies.

The Department of Agriculture estimated, in its Year Book of 1936, that 77,000,000 acres had been drained in the United States up until that point. The U.S. Fish and Wildlife Service, on the other hand, reported in its 1964 book *Waterfowl Tomorrow* that in the 1950's we still had some 82,000,000 acres of wetlands left from an estimated 127,000,000 acres which we once enjoyed.

The figures don't jibe, which isn't difficult to understand.

Draglines and bulldozers have done more to decrease waterfowl populations than all the hunters in the nation. Federal and state agencies, and to a lesser extent private industry, have drained a huge portion of the wetlands of this continent.

But the point is that massive loss of wetlands had occurred at those points, and the tragic aspect is that the rate of drainage has accelerated tremendously since those two points in time.

The extreme drought years in the early 1930's sent waterfowl production plummeting, and guesstimates of the total continental duck population during that low period was in the 30,000,000 range. Nature occasioned those population losses, however, and when the pendulum swung back to a rainy cycle, nature brought the birds back. The ponds and sloughs and marshes and potholes were still there, and when they were again filled with water the ducks came back.

The Dakotas and western Minnesota are the "duck factory" of the United States, far outranking all other areas in importance for duck production. This one area may at one time have produced 15,000,000 ducks each year, according to the U.S. Department of Agriculture (1955 Year Book—Tom Schrader). It was still in excellent condition to continue doing just that when the rains finally came in the late 1930's.

At that time, according to a survey taken by the U.S. Fish and Wildlife Service and state game departments, North Dakota still had about 664,000 potholes covering 2,152,000 acres; South Dakota, 422,000 potholes covering 817,000 acres; and Minnesota, 124,000 potholes covering 1,464,000 acres. That was a total, in this tri-state area, of 1,210,000 potholes covering 4,450,000 acres. It was a haven for ducks and a bonanza for duck hunters throughout the Mississippi and Central flyways.

Then came Uncle Sam, well-heeled with your tax dollars. The beginning of the end, or near-end, came in 1936, when Congress passed the Soil Conservation and Domestic Allotment Act. This was the basis for federal subsidization of many soil and water practices, and federal aid for drainage became a fact of life for this tri-state area in 1942.

The avowed purpose was to increase crop production during World War II, but it had little effect until after the war was ended. Far from being ended when the war ended, this subsidized drainage program really began to pick up momentum which continues until this day.

The U.S. Fish and Wildlife Service, concerned over wetland losses, began trying to stem the tide, but it was no contest. By 1956 the Service had bought 237,979 acres of wetlands. At that same point there had been 5,030,967 acres of land drained in the tri-state area alone.

The federal record has been a sorry one with respect to land management—in other words, in respect to resource management. For decades the U.S. government has, at one and the same time, paid farmers not to grow crops, paid them to drain and clear lands (to be placed into agricultural production), and guaranteed them a minimum price for products when they were produced. And millions of tax dollars have been paid to store surplus grains produced on lands which tax dollars helped drain.

H. R. Morgan said it well for the National Wildlife Federation in 1960 when he wrote: "Much of the pothole area of the tri-state region lies in marginal cropland country. The expenditure of public funds to convert it from the grassland economy for which the Almighty intended it to a rowcrop economy is a fallacy. This constitutes an area where zoning should be applied. Continued effort to perpetuate this land in a use for which Nature has not qualified it only puts off the day of reckoning, and perpetuates rural slums. Sooner or later we must pay the price when we refuse to 'use land according to its capabilities and treat it in accordance with its needs.' "

By the mid-1950's the mechanics and the machinery of drainage programs were well oiled, and the program rolled forward with awesome momentum. Governmental agencies involved with the program had honed their techniques of offering aid to landowners down to a fine point, and manufacturers of drainage equipment such as bulldozers and draglines worked hand in glove to expand and foster the projects.

The U.S. Soil Conservation Service is a particularly efficient organization, and has supplied the technical assistance, engineering services and general counseling which has resulted in the draining of millions of acres of private wetlands. Working closely with local soil conservation districts, it has stimulated requests from those districts for area-wide projects which have caused the draining of still more wetlands.

The move to drain wetlands and place them into agricultural production has reached the Canadian prairie provinces, and the pressure will continue to mount on all waterfowl production areas of this continent. Our détente with Russia and China, with the completed and predicted grain sales of huge proportions to those countries, can do nothing but stimulate more loss of wetlands.

The prairie pothole country of Canada is a semi-arid region with a history of wet and dry periods. Those drought years actually serve a purpose, allowing the soil to regenerate itself, and duck production is always excellent when water returns following such a dry period. If, that is, the wetlands haven't been ditched and drained during the interim.

Although a vast majority of the wetlands important for waterfowl are private lands, there was and is a critical need for both state, federal and provincial governments to acquire wetlands for the public. In 1961, Congress authorized a loan fund of $105,000,000 for such acquisition, with the money to be repaid from the sale of "duck stamps." The program has met with very modest success, and losses continue to outstrip gains by a wide margin.

Wintering grounds are important too

Although the waterfowl production areas, largely in the northern part of the U.S. and in Canada, are of utmost importance, the thrust of the fight to save them has largely obscured the value of the wintering grounds. If ducks and geese have nowhere to go when cold and ice and instinct sends them south, they are in serious trouble, as are the duck hunters of those southern areas.

California is the key wintering area for birds of the Pacific Flyway, and wetland losses there have been enormous. Of the estimated 5,000,000 acres of wetlands which existed there in the early history, some 3,500,000 acres were good waterfowl habitat.

By 1954 those wetlands had shrunk to 500,000 acres, and of those 300,000 acres are in privately owned duck clubs. It is graphic evidence of the importance of such clubs in main-

Without the wetlands in the nesting areas of Canada, hunters to the south would wait in vain for flights of ducks which would never appear. Ducks Unlimited and Canadian and U.S. governmental and state wildlife agencies are working to ensure that this does not happen.

taining waterfowl habitat. Of the remainder of the California wetlands, about 200,000 acres are in federal and state refuges, and half a million acres of seasonally flooded agricultural land provide good habitat for waterfowl.

Examples of the vital help which duck-hunting clubs provide in maintaining and preserving and enhancing duck and goose habitat on the wintering grounds can be found from coast to coast. Large estates along the South Carolina coast maintain marshes which are gunned only lightly. It is in the vast coastal marshes of Louisiana and Texas, however, where hunting itself has played and is playing such a vital role in keeping wetlands wet.

Literally millions of acres of these marshes remain in waterfowl habitat primarily because they are used for duck and goose hunting. Few of these acres actually belong to duck clubs, and the landowners make enough from duck and goose leases, from fur trapping and from alligator harvest, to justify keeping those acres in marsh.

Not all, of course. Hundreds of thousands of acres *have* been drained, much of it to be placed into improved pastures. Once the economic incentive of waterfowl leases is removed, if ever that comes to pass, millions of other acres will go that route. If that happens, the duck hunter will be the loser, but so will all of the ducks, geese, fur bearers, alligators and all the other creatures which require a wetland home.

Arkansas and Illinois and Missouri are other states where duck and goose clubs play a sizable role in providing winter waterfowl habitat. In Arkansas alone, more than 350 duck clubs manage more than 100,000 acres, much of it the artificially flooded green-tree-reservoir types which provide water even in dry years.

Drainage in the name of flood control has been disastrous for countless wetland areas, particularly in the Mississippi Flyway. The hardwood bottomland river swamps of Illinois, Iowa, Missouri, Arkansas, Louisiana, Tennessee and Mississippi have suffered enormously.

Such drainage is almost always followed by land clearing, with conversion to row crops the usual goal. More than a million acres in Louisiana alone have been cleared in the past decade, with most of it being planted to soybeans. Not all was waterfowl habitat, but the drainage required to dry up the land sufficiently for agricultural production effectively eliminated countless duck sloughs, brakes, lakes and overflow areas.

Following the great Mississippi River flood of 1927, Congress gave the Army Corps of Engineers authority to proceed with flood control projects on the entire river and its tributaries. The Corps has done quite a job—many consider it a misguided one—of leveeing off the backwater sump areas which once provided safety-valve overflow "reservoirs" from Illinois south to the Gulf. Most of those sump areas have been completely drained, a task made easy by the main-stem levees, and thus entirely removed from the waterfowl habitat picture.

The Corps is still embarked on this program, and last year

Where the habitat goes: Channelization of the lower Cache River, once prime winter waterfowl habitat, will eventually allow the whole river basin to be put into cultivation.

began a massive channelization project on Arkansas' Cache River which will destroy one of the finest waterfowl areas on the continent. Only an aroused, indignant public, putting far more pressure into congressional protests than has been the case up until now, will end this taxpayer-financed rape of the resource.

And enter the good guy turned villain—the Soil Conservation Service. It now has jurisdiction over the small watersheds of the nation, courtesy of a 1954 bill passed by Congress which is called the Watershed Protection and Flood Prevention Act (PL-566).

The main thrust of the SCS efforts under PL-566 has been toward channelization of streams. They take a meandering creek or river and convert it into a drainage ditch, whose bare, muddy banks slice with engineering precision in a straight line across the area. Swamps and marshes are drained in the process.

Such SCS projects have been completed from the Dakotas to Georgia and most points in between, and hundreds more are planned and authorized. In the southeastern states alone more than 25,000 miles of stream channels will be affected by projects planned and authorized.

Both houses of Congress have held hearings on stream channelization, and there is a mounting wave of concern about it. Most conservationists believe a complete moratorium on further ditching and dredging by public agencies should be placed into effect, to give the nation time to work out a plan for the salvation of our irreplaceable outdoor resources. From the standpoint of waterfowl, each day represents another bit of wetlands lost, as the drag lines grind away.

The damming of streams can also have adverse effect on waterfowl habitat. Hundreds of reservoirs have been built across the nation, and they typically flood a river bottom which provided duck and goose living quarters to a greater or lesser degree. For the pleasure of having these new lakes, which provide a great amount of outdoor recreation in the form of fishing and boating, we sacrifice wildlife habitat. In the consideration of each new lake proposal, these values should be carefully weighed against each other.

About the future

Better planning, bulwarked with massive public support, can ensure that we have a huntable population of wildfowl for many, many years. Despite the losses we have sustained in the past forty years where wetlands are concerned, and the inevitable continued loss of still more, I am hopeful that the public in general and hunters in particular will insist that this magnificent resource be maintained.

We are getting better planning, and better support from the public, and the two will hopefully result in a more adequate financing of our waterfowl management program. I am optimistic enough to believe that, within the next decade, this parlay will bring about an end to the indiscriminate destruction of wetlands by public agencies, or to such subsidized destruction by anyone.

The key question is how much wetlands we'll have left when this comes to pass, and that uncertainty underscores the urgency of the situation. There is no more time to waste.

Nobody can predict what the future holds for waterfowl, but it's a safe bet that ducks and geese will lose when their living requirements conflict with a real need of an expanding civilization. In most of the instances where we are now losing habitat that "need" does not exist.

When conversion of wetlands to agricultural production means the difference between food on the tables of this country and no food, the wetlands will go. But we are far, far from that point. The marvels of agricultural achievements have been able to produce more and more on less and less land, so much so that the nation has been able to retire from

Wherever they occur, wetlands benefit a host of wild creatures in addition to waterfowl, and each loss of this kind of habitat is a loss to many species. Furbearers like this nutria, alligators, and a great array of aquatic non-game birds also depend on wetlands for survival.

production millions of acres of land. Under such conditions it borders on the criminal for us to continue to drain wetlands for the purpose of agricultural production.

Both state governments and the federal government must continue to acquire wetlands as rapidly as possible, on an accelerated basis, for each year which passes places some of these out of reach. They become more valuable, in terms of dollars, for highways and shopping centers and housing developments than they are for ducks.

We'll lose more wetlands, but we're going to make some great strides forward in other areas, hopefully strides which will more than compensate. Continued research and management should end or minimize the loss of millions of wildfowl each year to lead poisoning, disease and pollution. I think we'll develop techniques for increasing substantially the duck production from a given area of marsh, and I'm excited about the prospects of developing breeding populations of ducks and geese in areas of the country where there are none now.

Education and training of hunters will reduce crippling losses in the coming years, adding still more millions of birds to the population remaining after the hunting seasons end.

The hunter should not expect to shoulder the burden of preserving and enhancing waterfowl habitat alone. The number of people who enjoy the federal refuges, state waterfowl refuges and private marshes are many times the number of waterfowl hunters, and these non-hunters should—and will, I believe—contribute to the financing this effort will require.

There is one other point which I hope hunters will keep ever before them. The sport hunter, per se, is probably the best friend that wildlife has. He has never been responsible for the extinction of any species, and has probably been responsible for the salvation of several.

But the sport hunter is not popular with a segment of the population of this nation, and the effort to end all hunting seems to be gathering momentum. The greatest mistake we who love wildfowling can make is to underestimate this movement. It is fueled with the same thread of sentimentality and misunderstanding and ignorance that have kept mourning doves off the legal hunting fare in some states.

Some of the leaders of the anti-hunting movement are on the far fringe of reason, but don't be misled into believing that all of them are. To the contrary, many members of the movement are quite sincere. They remain in the background, and they exist in huge numbers in the large cities where they have little or no access to the outdoors or to knowledge about it.

But they can vote, and such huge cities can swing the outcome of a state election. At some point down the line some such state election will include a referendum to end sport hunting. When that time comes you and I will, hopefully, have been able to educate enough of those city dwellers as to what is really best for the waterfowl resource: a continuing army of concerned, dedicated hunters who will spare no effort to ensure the continued well-being of wildlife.

The future? It could be great, but it *will be* what we make it.

Chapter 17

Cook 'Em with Kindness

"WILD GAME? I've never tasted any I liked, no matter how it was cooked."

Does that sound familiar! I've heard it many times over the years, and I'm certain it will be repeated many times in the future. There undoubtedly are some people who simply don't like a "wild" taste, whatever that is, but most who don't like any game at all just haven't eaten any which was properly prepared.

When elk or deer is cared for and cooked as it should be, their meat is frequently almost indistinguishable from beef. I have, in fact, eaten elk which I thought was beef. With such "game," then, there is little reason not to like it unless you don't like beef.

Ducks and geese are something else again, and they do have a different (perhaps it *is* wild) flavor. Ducks don't taste like chickens and geese don't taste like turkeys, and I find that a delightful situation. I like the distinctive flavor of these wildfowl, and prefer methods of cooking which enhance that flavor rather than conceal it.

But the flavor is different, and it is normal to expect that some people won't like ducks and geese no matter how they're handled. So be it!

Proper preparation of wild game begins the minute it's shot. As I said, I've eaten elk and thought it was beef, but I've certainly also eaten elk and thought it was awful. In most instances the difference was brought about by improper handling in the field.

The classic example of mishandling is the hunter who drapes a buck across the hood of his auto and drives a few hundred miles back home, often with an overnight stop enroute. Along the way that hunter may be treated to the envious glances of bystanders and other motorists, but his deer is also treated—to dust, dirt, auto fumes, insects and to the heat from his auto engine. The last influence is the worst, causing rapid deterioration of the meat.

I haven't seen anybody string their ducks or geese across the auto hood (yet), but it is possible to treat the birds almost as badly with a little effort. Just pile several limits together in the closed trunk of your car, leave it in the hot sun for half a day, and you'll bring about a noticeable change in the quality of your table fare. The change is all bad.

Fortunately, a modest amount of common sense is all that's required to properly care for any kind of game in the field, and with birds the task is infinitely easier than with big game. Nobody would stash a batch of undressed, dead chickens in a hot, closed area for hours before processing them, and ducks and geese deserve equally considerate care.

If the weather is cold, which is the normal situation for most duck and goose hunting situations in the United States and in Canada, no special handling of the kill is necessary if the birds are to be dressed back at camp that afternoon or night. If the weather is warm or hot, usually the situation in parts of Mexico, often the case in the southern part of the United States during the regular season, and always true during the special September teal seasons, it may be wise to take special precautions.

In hot weather, during a lull in the shooting, take a minute to field-dress the ducks and geese, removing the entrails. Even if the weather is only warm and you have quite a drive back to camp or town where the birds will be cleaned, field-dress them at the end of the shooting day.

The goal of your field-care efforts should be to cool the body heat from the birds as quickly as possible, and to keep that temperature down until the birds are cleaned.

The best way to clean ducks and geese is to talk your buddy into doing it. Next best is to pay a commercial duck picker to do the job, and you'll find a number of these around most key waterfowl-shooting centers. Locker plants frequently operate a duck and goose processing business along with their storage operations, which is a good combination. When you leave birds at one of these, leave with them a tag listing species and sex of the birds, date killed, and your name, address and hunting license number. It will be required at most, and is protection for you in any case.

I have picked hundreds of ducks and geese over the years, but experience doesn't seem to make me dislike the task any less. At the end of the shooting day, when the guns have been cleaned and placed in the rack, my druthers are to relax before the fireplace with a scotch and water and elaborate on the better shots I made that day, spicing the recital with original excuses for the misses.

I can remember one lone exception. Years ago some eight or ten of us made a three-day trip into the Atchafalaya swamp of southern Louisiana to hunt ducks, arriving at the camp about midafternoon. Confident of success, we took nothing to eat but the trimmings, depending upon mallard for the main dish. That included the first day's evening meal, so half the group immediately left camp to hunt while the rest unpacked and set up housekeeping.

Water levels in the Atchafalaya Basin fluctuate widely, and on that day reaching the backwaters where we hunted called for a several-mile hike through the bottomland timber, plus wading through the knee-deep, boggy water for as far as necessary to find ducks. When we had made the hike we found the area around Bay Denny ominously devoid of duck talk, of ducks, and of any evidence that ducks had been feeding thereabouts. No mallards! No wood ducks! No ducks!

Fueled by visions of hunger, Hurley Campbell and I kept slogging deeper and deeper into the swamp in search of supper, paralleling each other 100 yards apart to increase our chances. Our strident, pleading, begging calling produced nothing, but just before shooting time ran out a lone mallard hen made a pass high above the timber midway between us. Hurley and I propelled six carefully calculated shots into her path, and it's doubtful if any triggers were ever pulled with more intensity. It seemed that we had missed, but then that poor wing-tipped mallard slanted down.

On the way into the swamp it was difficult to walk, as we were sinking into mud about as deep as the water, but in some fashion Hurley and I reached the mallard about the time she hit the water. Desperation is a tremendous stimulant.

During the long walk out, after dark, we kept checking each other to make sure we didn't lose that one duck. And back at camp picking that hen was a labor of love. The gumbo was a bit thin, but spread over mountains of rice it was an epicurean masterpiece.

Okay, so you can't talk anybody else into picking them and there's no commercial picker around, which leaves only you. I make the task easier by dipping the birds very briefly into hot (almost boiling) water, the same way we always picked chickens when I was growing up. Purists insist that the

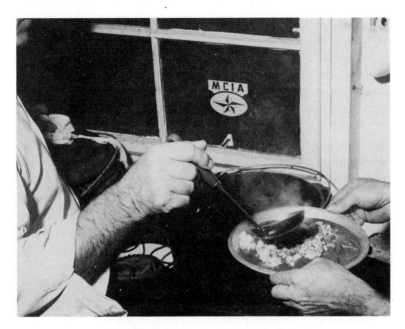

Duck gumbo gets a little thin when there's only one duck to feed the camp, but that's the beauty of duck gumbo—you can stretch the ducks to fit the occasion.

birds be drypicked, but I can't tell any difference once the birds are on the table.

Removing the outer feathers isn't too tough, but getting the down off can be a problem. A good method of coping with that is to melt paraffin and dip the birds into that. When the paraffin cools and hardens, you can break and peel it off and the down will come with it. You can reuse the paraffin by heating it and straining out the feathers and down.

Some people prefer to singe the down from their ducks, especially if there aren't enough birds involved to make the paraffin operation worth the effort. Don't make the mistake of singeing them over your gas burners inside the house, since the odor of burned feathers will linger long. Do it outside, over a camp stove or just over burning newspapers.

Transparent, plastic bags for individual ducks and geese are probably the best and easiest way to package them immediately after cleaning, unless they're to be cooked right then. If I'm to be back home in a day or two, I prefer not to freeze the birds until I get there. Caution: If you intend to keep ducks or geese in the freezer for any length of time, those plastic bags are not sufficient to prevent freezer burn. I routinely wrap each bird in its plastic bag with heavy freezer paper, sealing it with tape, and note on the package the date and contents.

If it seems that I'm making a federal case out of caring for waterfowl between the time they're shot and the time they're cooked, you're right. They're worth it. If you don't believe that, just add up the costs of your duck and goose hunting for the past season and compute the total down to a price per bird that ends up on your dining table. Then again, perhaps you shouldn't. I tend to shy away from such prosaic statistics.

Hanging ducks or geese in the raw to let them age was a favorite pastime in the distant past, and clings with us to a very limited extent. Best guess is that the practice began because there was no refrigeration, hence nothing else to do with the birds except to hang them. Some stout souls maintained that they should be hung by the heads until the carcasses fell to the ground. Only then were they properly aged. Hmmmm.

Hanging, in my opinion, is for horse thieves. Once the body heat of the birds is dissipated, I get mine into refrigeration of some kind as quickly as possible.

Skinning waterfowl instead of picking them lies somewhat in the category of "hanging." Hunters are rather rigidly divided into two schools of thought on the subject. If the bird is particularly gamy, and you want to eliminate some of that, skinning helps.

My rule of thumb is that I prefer the birds picked if they're to be roasted or cooked whole in some other manner, such as over charcoal or in a smoker. The skin helps keep them moist. If the ducks or geese are to be disjointed or cut into pieces for cooking, it doesn't seem to matter whether they're skinned or picked.

The flavor of waterfowl will vary from place to place and from species to species, which is as much to be expected as variations in grades of beef. Brant feeding on eelgrass are excellent, but when sea lettuce is their food they are virtually inedible. Canvasbacks whose diet has been one of wild celery are superb, but in the unusual situations where they are concentrating on fish and mollusc they are something less. Grain-fed mallards fresh from the cornfields, and pintails from the ricefields, leave little to be desired.

To the kitchen

Each time I have duck for dinner I'm inclined to believe that's the best I've ever eaten, but that only indicates that I like ducks and geese. In this chapter I'm giving you some of my favorite recipes, most of which you'll find extremely simple.

During almost three decades of life with me as the wife of an Air Force instructor, student, biologist, refuge manager and outdoor writer, Mary has had occasion to cook a wide array of wild critters, often under unusual conditions, and sometimes from necessity. With the possible exception of the fried rattlesnake she has come through with flying colors. She is, in fact, the best cook I know, so I'll save a couple of her best recipes for last.

Ducks coming from the oven at the Oak Grove Hunting Club at Creole, Louisiana. One duck per man is the "ration" at a duck dinner there, and it never seems to be too much.

Smoked ducks and geese

This is my thing. Our Char-Broil barbecue pit has a smoker attachment which permits it to do wondrous things to any piece of meat, including waterfowl. Ducks and geese smoked in the fashion outlined below are great as the main dish of a meal, but we frequently prefer them as hors d'oeuvres. Slice the meat in slivers and serve during the cocktail hour.

Line the top of your charcoal grill with heavy aluminum foil, turning the edges up to form a shallow pan. This will prevent the drippings from falling through the grating, and eliminate a messy cleaning job.

Grease the outside of the birds lightly with cooking oil, then salt and pepper well both inside and out. Place them on the foil breast up, and drape across each two to four slices of bacon, depending upon the size of the bird. As they slowly cook, grease from the bacon will automatically baste the birds, but go one step farther and make up a batch of my super-simple "Grits' Game Sauce": melted margarine, lemon juice and salt and pepper, in proportions to suit your particular tastes. You can't go wrong, since it turns out either good, better or best each time.

The smoker will keep the temperature of the Char-Broil at from 200 to 450 degrees, depending upon where you have set the damper. I prefer it down around 250 to 350. It will fluctuate somewhat from one charcoal refill to the next, which doesn't matter.

Smoke cooking requires a long time, so don't do it if you're in a hurry. Allow six to twelve hours, depending upon how big the birds are and how hot your grill is. The beauty of this brand of cooking is that it requires so little attention. Just check every hour or two or three, add charcoal when necessary, and baste with GGS whenever you happen to be passing by.

The birds are ready when they're cooked the way you like

them. I prefer mine rare to medium-rare, but let your taste buds be your guide. Those taste buds should also determine whether or not you add hickory chips to your smoking fire.

When serving the smoked birds as hors d'oeuvres, include on the tray a bottle of Tabasco. Encourage your guests to add one drop of the hot stuff per sliver of smoked duck or goose, and then request a brief moment of silence during which all can give thanks for being privy to anything that good.

Charcoaled ducks

This is my other thing. Here the ducks are placed on a spit and cooked directly over charcoal, but again with the hood down. Arrange the charcoal in two lines parallel to the spit and a bit to either side. Keep the spit rotating, and make sure the skewers keep the birds turning with the spit.

Prepare the birds just as above for smoking, but in this case pin the strips of bacon around them with toothpicks to prevent them from falling off as the spit turns. Use a medium fire and baste frequently with GGS.

Wag's fried duck

A dandy from Wag's Game Preserve, Royal, Arkansas. Cut the meat from breasts of ducks, and cut off legs and thighs together. Salt and pepper well, then marinate for one hour in vegetable oil and two cloves of crushed garlic. Remove from the marinade and fry quickly for about five minutes. This is best served rare with Wag's Shotgun Sauce, which is made like this: In an iron skillet place one part butter to two parts currant or muscadine jelly and add a dash of Worcestershire sauce. Heat and stir, and serve when hot.

Mary Land's spaghetti with duck

Mary Land, one of my favorite people, lives just down the river from me. She is an experienced outdoorswoman, talented artist, accomplished musician and composer, and an excellent writer, and numbered among her accomplishments under the latter category are two fine books titled *Mary Land's Louisiana Cookery* and *New Orleans Cuisine*. I want to share with you this treat of hers.

Sauté one cup of minced shallots, one cup of minced green peppers and one pod of garlic in butter. Remove garlic. Add twelve fresh, peeled tomatoes, a pinch of oregano, salt and cayenne, three cans of mushrooms and two bay leaves. Simmer thirty minutes. Add slices of one cooked duck to this sauce and let them remain in sauce thirty minutes, then remove the bay leaves. Boil one pound of Italian spaghetti in water for ten minutes, and rinse under cold, running water. Drain and place in a bowl. Pour hot sauce over the spaghetti and sprinkle with Parmesan cheese.

Another dandy Mary Land special is her breast of goose. Just slice the cooked breast of a goose and serve it cold with a wine sauce. Or serve with brandy poured over it and lighted, being sure to heat the brandy before pouring.

Duck gumbo

There is no one way to make a gumbo, just as there is no one way to make a soup, but the beauty is that the worst gumbo is better than most of us deserve. It is properly served over mounds of fluffy rice.

One or two ducks	2 tablespoons flour
1 fresh tomato, chopped	3 quarts water
1½ pounds fresh okra	3 tablespoons shortening or
1 large onion, chopped	bacon drippings
2 tablespoons shortening	3 cloves garlic
Salt and pepper	½ bell pepper

Cut the ducks up, salt and pepper the pieces well, roll in flour and fry until brown. Fry okra, onion, garlic and chopped bell pepper in the shortening. Make a roux in a heavy skillet, using grease from fried duck and flour. Add the fried duck and the vegetables, stir for a few minutes, and then add the water. The amount of water will determine how thick the gumbo is, and can be varied to suit individual preference. Salt and pepper to taste, and cook slowly for about two hours.

There are many variations. Filé (powdered sassafras) can be used instead of the okra, adding about a teaspoon just before or just after the gumbo is removed from the heat. Some prefer to omit the garlic, and I frequently add a few oysters and shrimp.

That "roux" is the basis for many, many dishes, as witnessed by the preface to many recipes: "First you make a roux." Make it by slowly sprinkling flour into a hot skillet of grease (or melted butter or shortening), stirring constantly. Brown very slowly until flour and fat are a dark brown, being careful not to burn it. From that point you can add whatever spices, herbs and other ingredients that make you happy, including hot water.

Roast specklebelly goose

Salt and pepper well and place a whole onion inside the cavity. Cook in the oven, in a covered roaster with a little water, at 500° for thirty minutes. Reduce heat to 300° and cook for one to two hours (until the fork comes out clean). Remove roaster cover, turn oven to broil, and cook until the skin on the breast of the goose crinkles up.

This is a super recipe taught me years ago by R. J. Stine and his wife. It works beautifully with other species of geese, juggling the timing for the variations in size. With Canada geese a good trick is to add a few strips of bacon inside with the onion, since Canadas tend to be a bit dry.

Mary's wild duck

Here's a favorite which my Mary has been concocting for years, from the *River Road Recipes.*

2 ducks	1 cup sherry
2 onions	1 tablespoon flour
1 rib celery	¼ cup water
¼ cup salad oil	3 tablespoons chopped parsley
1 cup water	Salt and pepper to taste

Salt and pepper ducks well inside and out, and place half an onion and half a rib of celery into each cavity. Brown ducks in open, heavy roasting pan at 400° in the oil. Wilt the chopped second onion in the fat around the ducks, then add a cup of water and a cup of sherry. Reduce heat to 350°, cover and cook until done. Baste and add more liquid if needed. Toward the end make a paste of flour and water and add this to the drippings. Add the chopped parsley, and more sherry if desired.

Mary's fricasseed duck

One or two ducks	3 cups water
4 tablespoons shortening	1 can mushroom sauce
4 tablespoons flour	Salt and pepper
¾ cup chopped onions	Seasoned salt

Cut the ducks into pieces, salt and pepper them, dip in flour and brown in a heavy skillet. Remove the ducks. Make a roux in the skillet by browning the flour in the shortening (or bacon drippings). Add and sauté the onions. Add water, mushroom sauce, seasoned salt, salt and pepper to taste. Cover the skillet and simmer until done, which will require an hour or two depending upon the size of the duck pieces.

Snipe à la Natchitoches

Place snipe on skewer of charcoal grill, separating each bird with several squares of bacon. Make sure birds and bacon are pushed tightly together on the skewer, so the bacon drippings will baste the snipe as they turn. Cook over a low charcoal fire until done, basting frequently with the standard Grits' Game Sauce of margarine, lemon juice, salt and pepper.

This is a superb recipe for other small birds such as doves, quail and woodcock.

Mary's Steamed Rice

Bring two cups of salted water to a boil, then add one cup of washed rice. Reduce heat and cook until the rice grains begin to soften. Place a tight lid on the boiler, and *then* remove it from the fire. Don't open until it has steamed for ten minutes.

A gimmick which Mary uses is to add a dash of oil or butter to the boiling water before adding the rice, which keeps it from boiling over. Stir the rice frequently as it boils. This recipe is virtually fail-safe.

No meal is more greatly enhanced by the serving of a good wine than one where waterfowl is the entrée. Red wine, white wine, chilled or room temperature . . . let your preference be your guide.

EPILOGUE

MEMORIES!

When I was only four years old, a favorite uncle gave me my first air rifle as a Christmas present, and that first BB gun was the forerunner of many more to follow. For me that gift from Uncle Leonard was the magic touch, and he must have realized that since he gave me another air rifle six months later, a pattern which continued for several years. It was a nice happenstance that my birthday came around each June, which made for perfect midyear spacing.

That was some forty-five years ago, which doesn't miss half a century by very much, and in that span of time the outdoors has been a way of life for me. It has been my thing, and still is, simply because I love it. It fills a need, beautifully.

Duck hunter's dream? No, but it might be—actually, these mallards dropped in to tell the Arkansas Game and Fish Commission that they liked its W. H. Claypool Reservoir in northeast Arkansas.

"Pick out one bird! Just one bird!" The words of Roy Ramage whirled in my mind as the covey of quail exploded in a blur of brown before the nose of old Dot. Part of that moving mass swung to my side and, glory be, there *was* that one bird . . . for the first time. As if an abruptly focused photograph on a screen, the cock bobwhite came into being, white face patch shining in the late-afternoon sun. When the slim tube of my single-barrel .410 passed that outstretched head I pulled the trigger, and watched in slow-motion fascination the fall of shot-stilled wings. It was quite a moment for a ten-year-old, as vivid today as then.

When dawn came Joe Blackburn and I were at about 8,000 feet, down quite a bit from our dry camp up above, and were settled just below the crest of a knife ridge. Far below the faint ribbon of the Middle Fork of Idaho's Salmon River twisted its way toward the sea. Fog swirled slowly down in the canyon, and a raven rode the air currents just above that white mass.

The incredible vastness of our Rockies is awe-inspiring, and never more so, to me, than during the stillness which blankets the land just before sunrise. The nearest road to the ridge where Joe and I sat was two days away to the east, by horseback, and as the light level increased the unending ridges and ranges which came into view accentuated the remoteness and isolation of that treasured spot.

It was a cathedral, no less, hardly susceptible of improvement. But then came the sound for which we had been waiting, the marvelous call of a bull elk. That wild whistle floated up from down the ridge, perfect orchestration for the scene, and sent chills up and down my spine.

We never saw that elk, but the memory lingers on. And so do the chills.

I have a mother lode of memories of just such moments, gathered from here and there around the world in a few decades of hunting and fishing. There was the stalk into the middle of a herd of Cape buffalo in Kenya, when I discovered just how huge a bull buff seems at fifteen yards. And the two leopards fighting around the base of the bait tree, forty yards from my blind.

Snowbird Lake in the Northwest Territories on the Fourth of July, standing on ice three feet thick and catching lake trout on a fly rod . . . the anticipation of a bass strike on a surface lure being twitched around the knees of a cypress tree in a Louisiana swamp . . . sea-run coho salmon in British Columbia's Kwatna River . . .

The variety of fare offered by the outdoors to the sportsman is immense, and to my way of thinking the individual items can only be catalogued as good, better, and best. I like it all, in short, but with no hesitation place waterfowl hunting in that "best" category. It has a flavor all its own.

Ducks and geese require wetlands, and this specialized requirement makes them especially vulnerable to the march of civilization. Without wetlands there would be no ducks and no geese, a point which has been made in several chapters in this book. The work being done to ensure preservation of aquatic habitat has been discussed, too, largely in the chapters on Ducks Unlimited and on waterfowl management, and I honestly believe such efforts will be moderately successful over the long haul. But I also reflect now and then as to the consequences if those efforts aren't successful, which always reminds me of this tale.

It seems that an avid duck hunter passed from this mortal scene to find that his wayward earthly ways had programmed him to Hell rather than to Heaven. To his great surprise he was made welcome that first morning with a duck hunt on the finest marsh he had ever seen. The equipment was the best—gun, blind, decoys, retriever, and Satan himself did the calling with unbelievable realism. But after several hours he had not seen a bird.

"This is beautiful," the duck hunter told his host, "but where are the ducks?"

"That's the Hell of it," replied Satan. "There aren't any."

No ducks. No geese. Can you imagine the emptiness of a world without them? No sound in the night of a flock of migrating geese overhead. No flock of mallards to follow a ladder of notes down to the blind. No bluebills to pour in over your blocks through the swirling snow.

The world wouldn't end, of course, but how much poorer it would be. Let's not let that happen.

Bibliography

Comparing notes about wildfowling is part of the fun, and reading about it can be even more entertaining and instructive than talking about it. The literature is so large that it's hard to know where to stop, and the following list is far from complete. It does, however, include most of the substantial current books, plus a few of the classics and out-of-print favorites that are so good, or so important, that they deserve inclusion on any list, just on general principles.

CURRENT GENERAL BOOKS

(Not all currently in print, but all published since World War II, and available with a little searching.)

Bauer, Erwin. *The Duck Hunter's Bible.* Garden City: Doubleday, 1965.

Becker, A. C., Jr. *Waterfowl in the Marshes.* New York: A. S. Barnes & Co., 1969.

Bernsen, Paul S. *The North American Waterfowler.* Seattle: Salisbury Press, 1972.

Heilner, Van Campen. *A Book of Duck Shooting.* New York: Alfred A. Knopf, 1947.

Holland, Ray P. *Shotgunning in the Lowlands.* New York: A. S. Barnes, 1945.

Janes, Edward C. *Hunting Ducks and Geese.* Harrisburg: Stackpole, 1964.

Labisky, Wallace. *Waterfowl Shooting.* New York: Greenberg, 1954.

MacKenty, John G. *Duck Hunting.* New York: A. S. Barnes, 1964.

Rice, F. P., and Dahl, J. I. *Game Bird Hunting.* New York: Harper & Row, 1965.

Scharff, Robert. *Complete Duck Shooter's Handbook.* New York: G. P. Putnam's Sons, 1957.

Note: Do not overlook the excellent material on wildfowling that is included in Raymond R. Camp's *The Hunter's Encyclopedia,* published by Stackpole. The articles aren't signed, but they were contributed by men like H. Albert Hochbaum, C. E. Gillham, C. E. ("Shang") Wheeler and Van Campen Heilner, and that's good enough for me.

IDENTIFICATION MANUALS

There are many modest but still generally satisfactory "quickie" identification charts available, not the least of which is the Government Printing Office's one-sheet, one-color chart which many fish & game departments distribute for no charge. The following manuals are more substantial, all featuring color pictures and including the less common wildfowl. Every duck hunter should own at least one of them.

Peterson, Roger Tory. *A Field Guide to the Birds,* Vol. 1. Boston: Houghton Mifflin, 1947.

Ruthven, J. A. and Zimmerman, Wm. *Top Flight Speed Index to Waterfowl of North America.* Milwaukee: Moebius Press, 1965.

Scott, Peter. *A Coloured Key to the Wildfowl of the World.* Slimbridge, England: Wildfowl Trust, 1957.

Sprunt, A., IV and Zim, H. S. *Gamebirds.* New York: Golden Press, 1961. (A marvelous value. Includes color pictures, distribution charts and all upland game species as well.)

BOOKS ON ONE OR MORE OF THE BIRDS THEMSELVES

Hall, Dr. Henry M. *A Gathering of Shore Birds.* New York: Devin-Adair, 1960.

Hochbaum, H. Albert. *The Canvasback on a Prairie Marsh.* Washington: American Wildlife Institute, 1944.

———. *Travels and Traditions of Waterfowl.* Minneapolis: University of Minnesota Press, 1955.

Johnsgard, Paul A. *Handbook of Waterfowl Behavior.* Ithaca: Cornell University Press, 1965.

———. *Waterfowl, Their Biology and Natural History.* Lincoln: University of Nebraska Press, 1968. (Includes photographs of most of the waterfowl of the world, many in color.)

Kortright, F. H. *The Ducks, Geese and Swans of North America.* Harrisburg: Stackpole, 1967. (Very comprehensive. Includes pictures of juvenile and eclipse plumages.)

Linduska, J. P. (ed.) *Waterfowl Tomorrow.* Washington: Government Printing Office, 1964.

Madson, John. *The Mallard.* East Alton: Olin Conservation Dept., 1963.

Phillips, J. C. *The Natural History of Ducks.* Boston: Houghton Mifflin, 1922–26. (In 4 volumes—a mammoth achievement, the definitive work.)

Williams, C. S. *Honker.* New York: D. Van Nostrand, 1967.

SHOTGUNS AND SHOTGUNNING

Most of the "complete" shooting and hunting books include material on wildfowling, some of it very good. These are excluded from the following list, which is limited to fairly current books dealing only with the scattergun which contain material of special value to waterfowlers.

Askins, Col. Charles. *The Shotgunner's Book.* Harrisburg: Stackpole, 1958.

Boughan, Rolla B. *Shotgun Ballistics for Hunters.* New York: A. S. Barnes, 1965.

Burrard, Maj. Sir Gerald. *The Modern Shotgun.* New York: A. S. Barnes, 1964.

Garwood, G. T. *Gough Thomas's Gun Book.* New York: Winchester Press, 1971.

———. *Gough Thomas's Second Gun Book.* New York: Winchester Press, 1972.

Keith, Elmer. *Shotguns by Keith.* Harrisburg: Stackpole, 1967.

Oberfell, G. G. and Thompson, C. E. *The Mysteries of Shotgun Patterns.* Stillwater: Oklahoma State University Press, 1960.

O'Connor, Jack. *The Shotgun Book.* New York: Alfred A. Knopf, 1965.

Sell, Francis. *The American Shotgunner.* Harrisburg: Stackpole, 1962.

DECOYS AND DECOY MAKING AND COLLECTING

Barber, Joel. *Wild Fowl Decoys.* New York: Dover, 1954.

Burk, Bruce. *Game Bird Carving.* New York: Winchester Press, 1972.

Connett, Eugene V., III. *Duck Decoys.* Brattleboro: Stephen Greene, 1953.

Coykendall, Ralf. *Duck Decoys and How to Rig Them.* New York: Holt, Rinehart & Winston, 1955.

Earnest, Adele. *The Art of the Decoy.* New York: Clarkson N. Potter, 1965.

Mackey, William J. *American Bird Decoys.* New York: E. P. Dutton, 1965.

Parmalee, P. W., and Loomis, F. D. *Decoys and Decoy Carvers of Illinois.* DeKalb: Northern Illinois University Press, 1969.

BOOKS ON RETRIEVERS AND RETRIEVER TRAINING

Duffey, David M. *Hunting Dog Know-How.* New York: Winchester Press, 1972.

Falk, John. *The Practical Hunter's Dog Book.* New York: Winchester Press, 1971.

Morgan, Charles. *Charles Morgan on Retrievers.* New York: Abercrombie & Fitch, 1968.

Wolters, Richard A. *Water Dog.* New York: E. P. Dutton, 1964.

REGIONAL BOOKS OF IMPORTANCE

Camp, Raymond R. *Duck Boats: Blinds: Decoys and Eastern Seaboard Wildfowling.* New York: Alfred A. Knopf, 1952.

Connett, Eugene V., III. *Duck Shooting Along the Atlantic Tidewater.* New York: William Morrow, 1947.

———. *Wildfowling in the Mississippi Flyway.* New York: D. Van Nostrand, 1949.

Elman, R. and Osborne, W. *The Atlantic Flyway.* New York: Winchester Press, 1972.

Walsh, Roy E. *Gunning the Chesapeake.* Cambridge: Tidewater, 1960.

NATURE PHOTOGRAPHY

Bauer, Erwin. *Outdoor Photography.* New York: Harper & Row, 1965.

Kine, Russ. *The Complete Book of Nature Photography.* New York: A. S. Barnes, 1962.

IMPORTANT OLDER BOOKS, AND BOOKS OF HISTORICAL INTEREST

Bogardus, Adam H. *Field, Cover and Trap Shooting.* New York: J. B. Ford, 1874.

Bruette, William A. *American Duck, Goose and Brant Shooting.* New York: G. H. Watt, 1929.

Grinnell, George B. *American Duck Shooting.* New York: Forest & Stream, 1901.

Hazelton, W. C. *Tales of Duck and Goose Shooting.* Chicago: Hazelton, 1916.

[Herbert, W. H.] *Frank Forester's Field Sports of the United States.* New York: Stringer & Townsend, 1849.

Hinman, Bob. *The Golden Age of Shotgunning.* New York: Winchester Press, 1971.

Kimball, D. and J. *The Market Hunter.* Minneapolis: Dillon Press, 1969.

Krider, John. *Krider's Sporting Anecdotes.* Philadelphia: A. Hart, 1853.

Leffingwell, W. B. *The Art of Wing Shooting.* Chicago: Rand McNally, 1894.

————. *Wild Fowl Shooting.* Chicago: Rand McNally, 1888.

Lewis, Elisha J. *The American Sportsman.* New York: Lippincott, 1857.

Long, Joseph W. *American Wild-Fowl Shooting.* New York: Orange, Judd, 1879.

Phillips, J. C. and Hill, L. W. *Classics of the American Shooting Field.* Boston: Houghton Mifflin, 1930.

Walsh, Harry M. *The Outlaw Gunner.* Cambridge: Tidewater, 1971.

Index